CROSSING
THE
THRESHOLD
OF
HOPE

*Translated from the Italian
by Jenny McPhee and Martha McPhee*

CROSSING
THE
THRESHOLD
OF
HOPE

by His Holiness
JOHN PAUL II

Edited by Vittorio Messori

*Published by Random House Large Print
in association with Alfred A. Knopf, Inc.
New York   1995*

Published simultaneously in Italy as *Varcare la Soglia della Speranza* by Giovanni Paolo II with an introduction by Vittorio Messori.

ISBN: 0-679-75868-2
LC: 94-78675

Manufactured in the United States of America
FIRST LARGE PRINT PAPERBACK EDITION

This Large Print Book carries the Seal of Approval of N.A.V.H.

How This Book
Came to Be

I<small>N</small> O<small>CTOBER</small> <small>OF</small> 1993 J<small>OHN</small> P<small>AUL</small> II <small>WOULD</small> complete fifteen years of his papacy. For the occasion the Holy Father accepted Italian Radio and Television's proposal for a televised interview that would be transmitted by the major networks around the world. It would have been the first ever in the history of the papacy, a history which, over the centuries, has experienced just about everything. But never before had a successor to Peter participated in a live televised interview with a journalist whose questions were entirely of his own making.

I was told that I had been chosen to conduct the interview because of the many religious books—especially *The Ratzinger Report* (1985)—and articles I have written over the years, with the freedom of a layman, but also as a believer who knows that the Church is given not only to the clergy but to each of the baptized.

The Pope, however, did not take into consideration how relentless his schedule would be in September, which was the deadline for filming, and allowed enough time for the director and technicians to work on the material before the broadcast. In the end, the Pope's many obligations prevented his participation and the project fell through at the last moment.

A few months passed. Then one day another telephone call came from the Vatican—again entirely unforeseen. On the line was the Press Secretary for the Holy See, Dr. Joaquín Navarro-Valls, a very efficient, cordial, friendly Spanish psychiatrist who had gone into journalism and who had been one of the staunchest supporters of the interview. Dr. Navarro-Valls was the bearer of a message that (he assured me) had surprised even him. The Pope, he said, sent him to say: "Even if there wasn't a way to respond to you in person, I kept your questions on my desk. They interested me. I didn't think it would be wise to let them go to waste. So I thought about them and, after some time, during the brief moments when I was free from obligations, I responded to them in writing. You have asked me questions, therefore you have a right to responses. . . . I am working on them. I will let you have them. Then do with them what you think is appropriate."

Once again John Paul II confirmed his reputation for being "the Pope of surprises"—an attribute that has characterized him from the time of his election, which upset all predictions.

One day at the end of April 1994, during a meeting in my house with Dr. Navarro-Valls, he pulled from his briefcase a big white envelope. Inside was the text I had been told about, straight from the hands of the Pope himself. He had vigorously underlined many points—which the reader will find italicized in the text, according to the instructions of the author. Likewise, the space breaks separating one paragraph from another are also preserved. The title of the book was chosen by John Paul II. He wrote it himself on the cover of the folder containing his manuscript, specifying, however, that this was only a suggestion and that he would leave it up to the editors to make the final decision on the book's title. We decided to keep his title exactly as written because we realized that it perfectly identified the heart of the message these pages convey.

A dutiful respect for a text in which every word counts obviously guided me in the editing work I was requested to do. I limited myself to the translation of Latin expressions, which appear in parentheses; to minimal readjustments in the punctuation; to the completion of proper names; to the suggestion of a synonym where a word was repeated in the same paragraph; and to the modification of some—rare—inaccuracies in the translation from the original Polish. Minutiae that in no way altered the content.

Introducing new questions into the text where needed was my most significant task. In fact, my original list of questions numbered only twenty. John Paul II had answered them with surprising diligence, without avoiding one of them. The fact that he had taken a journalist so seriously is yet more proof—if there were ever a need—of his humility, of his generous availability to hear our voices, those of the common "Christians on the street."

The text, which will be published in Italy and simultaneously in all the major languages of the world, was examined and approved by the author himself. It is my duty to guarantee to the reader that the voice that resonates—in its humanity but also in its authority—is entirely that of the successor to Peter. It will now be the job of theologians and analysts of the papal teaching to face the problem of classifying a text that has no precedent and therefore poses new possibilities for the Church.

Above all else, the pages that follow make it clear that this is a Pope who is impatient in his apostolic zeal; a shepherd to whom the usual paths always seem insufficient; who looks for every means to spread the Good News to men; who—evangelically—wants to shout from the rooftops (today crowded with television antennae) that there is hope, that it has been confirmed, that it is offered to whoever wants to accept it. Even a conversation with a journalist is valued by this Pope as part of the tradition of Paul in the First Letter to the Corinthians: "I have become all things to all, to save at least some. All this I do for the sake of the gospel, so that I too may share in it" (1 Cor 9:22–23).

In such a climate all abstractions vanish. Dogma becomes flesh, blood, life. The theologian becomes witness and shepherd.

Vittorio Messori

CROSSING
THE
THRESHOLD
OF
HOPE

"The Pope":
A Scandal and
a Mystery

Y OUR HOLINESS, MY FIRST QUESTION WILL go right to the point. Therefore, please understand if it is longer than those that follow.

In front of me is a man dressed in the white of ancient custom, with a cross over his chest. This man who is called the *Pope* (from "father," in Greek) is a mystery in and of himself, a sign of contradiction. He is even considered a challenge or a "scandal" to logic or good sense by many of our contemporaries.

Confronted with the Pope, one must make a choice. The leader of the Catholic Church is defined by the faith as the Vicar of Jesus Christ (and is accepted as such by believers). The Pope is considered the man on earth who represents the Son of God, who "takes the place" of the Second Person of the omnipotent God of the Trinity.

Each Pope regards his role with a sense of duty and humility, of course, but also with an equal sense of confidence. Catholics believe this and therefore they call him "Holy Father" or "Your Holiness."

Nevertheless, according to many others, this is an absurd and unbelievable claim. The Pope, for them, is not God's representative. He is, instead, the surviving witness of ancient myths and legends that today the "adult" does not accept.

Confronted with you—as with each of your predecessors and successors—one must wager, as Pascal said, that you are either the mysterious living proof of the Creator of the universe or the central protagonist of a millennial illusion.

May I ask: Have you ever once hesitated in your belief in your relationship with Jesus Christ and therefore with God? Haven't you ever had, not doubts certainly, but at least questions and problems (as is human) about the truth of this *Creed* which is repeated at each Mass and which proclaims an unprecedented faith, of which you are the highest guarantor?

M Y EXPLANATION BEGINS BY CLARIFYING words and concepts. Your question is infused with both a lively faith and a certain anxiety. I state right from the outset: "Be not afraid!" This is the same exhortation that resounded at the beginning of my ministry in the See of Saint Peter.

Christ addressed this invitation many times to those He met. The angel said to Mary: "Be not afraid!" (cf. Lk

1:30). The same was said to Joseph: "Be not afraid!" (cf. Mt 1:20). Christ said the same to the apostles, to Peter, in various circumstances, and especially after His Resurrection. He kept telling them: "Be not afraid!" He sensed, in fact, that they were afraid. They were not sure if who they saw was the same Christ they had known. They were afraid when He was arrested; they were even more afraid after his Resurrection.

The words Christ uttered are repeated by the Church. *And with the Church, they are repeated by the Pope.* I have done so since the first homily I gave in St. Peter's Square: "Be not afraid!" These are not words said into a void. They are profoundly rooted in the Gospel. They are simply the words of Christ Himself.

Of what should we not be afraid? We should not fear *the truth about ourselves.* One day Peter became aware of this and with particular energy he said to Jesus: "Depart from me, Lord, for I am a sinful man" (Lk 5:8).

Peter was not the only one who was aware of this truth. Every man has learned it. Every successor to Peter has learned it. I learned it very well. Every one of us is *indebted to Peter* for what he said on that day: "Depart from me, Lord, for I am a sinful man." Christ answered him: "Do not be afraid; from now on you will be catching men" (Lk 5:10). *Do not be afraid of men!* Man is always the same. The systems he creates are always imperfect, and the more imperfect they are, the more he is sure of himself. Where does this originate? It comes from the human heart. Our hearts are anxious. Christ knows our anguish best of all: "Christ knows that which is in every man" (cf. Jn 2:25).

Returning to your question, I would like to recall the words of Christ together with my first words in St. Peter's Square: "Be not afraid." Have no fear when people call me the "Vicar of Christ," when they say to me "Holy Father," or "Your Holiness," or use titles similar to these, which seem even inimical to the Gospel. Christ himself declared: "Call no one on earth your father; you have but one Father in heaven. Do not be called 'Master'; you have but one master, the Messiah" (Mt 23:9–10). These expressions, nevertheless, have evolved out of a long tradition, becoming part of common usage. One must not be afraid of these words either.

Every time Christ exhorts us to have no fear, He has both God and man in mind. He means: *Do not be afraid of God,* who, according to philosophers, is the transcendent Absolute. Do not be afraid of God, but invoke Him with me: "Our Father" (Mt 6:9). *Do not be afraid to say "Father"!* Desire to be perfect just as He is, because He is perfect. "So be perfect, just as your heavenly Father is perfect" (Mt 5:48).

Christ is the *sacrament of the invisible God*—a sacrament that indicates presence. God is with us. God, infinitely perfect, is not only with man, but He Himself became a man in Jesus Christ. *Do not be afraid of God who became a man!* It was precisely this that Peter said at Caesarea Philippi: "You are the Messiah, the Son of the living God" (Mt 16:16). Indirectly He affirmed: You are the Son of God who became a man. Peter was not afraid to say it, even if these words did not come from him. They came from the Father. "No one knows the Son except the Father, and no one knows the Father except the Son" (cf. Mt 11:27).

"Blessed are you, Simon son of Jonah. For flesh and blood has not revealed this to you, but my heavenly Father" (Mt 16:17). Peter uttered these words through the power of the Holy Spirit. The Church also continues to utter them through the power of the Holy Spirit.

Peter was not afraid of God who had become a man. *He was afraid, instead, for the Son of God as a man.* Peter could not accept that He would be whipped and crowned with thorns and finally crucified. Peter could not accept that. He was afraid. And for this Christ severely *reproached him,* but He did not *reject him.*

Peter had goodwill and a fervent heart and Christ did not reject him, this man who at Gethsemane even drew his sword in order to defend his Master. Jesus only said to him: "Simon, Simon, behold Satan has demanded to sift all of you like wheat, but I have prayed . . . and once you have turned back, you must strengthen your brothers" (cf. Lk 22:31–32). Christ did not reject Peter; He valued his profession of faith at Caesarea Philippi and, with the power of the Holy Spirit, He led him through His Passion and beyond his denial.

Peter, as a man, demonstrated that he was not capable of following Christ everywhere, and especially not to death. After the Resurrection, however, he was the first of the apostles to realize, together with John, that Christ's body was not in the tomb.

Even after the Resurrection, Christ confirmed Peter's mission. He said meaningfully: "Feed my lambs. . . . Tend my sheep" (Jn 21:15–16). But first Christ asked if Peter loved Him. Peter, who had denied Christ but had not stopped loving Him, was able to respond: "You know that I love you" (Jn 21:15). But he did not say again: "Even though I should have to die with you, I will not deny you" (Mt 26:35). *It was no longer only a question of Peter,* and of his simple human strengths; it had become by now a question of the Holy Spirit, promised by Christ to the one who would take His place on earth.

On the day of Pentecost, Peter was the first to speak to the gathered Israelites and to others who had traveled various distances. He reminded them of the wrong committed by those who had nailed Christ to the Cross, and then He confirmed His Resurrection. He exhorted the people to conversion and to baptism. Thanks to the work of the Holy Spirit, *Christ could have confidence in Peter,* He could *lean on him*—on him and on all the other apostles—even on Paul, who still persecuted Christians and hated the name Jesus.

Against this background, a historical background, expressions such as "Supreme Pontiff," "Your Holiness," and "Holy Father" are of little importance. What is important originates in the Death and Resurrection of Christ. What is important is that which comes from the power of the Holy Spirit. For example, Peter, together with the other apostles, and (after his conversion) Paul became *authentic witnesses of Christ, faithful unto the shedding of their blood.*

Peter did not further deny Christ and he never repeated his unfortunate statement: "I do not know the man" (Mt 26:72). *He persevered in his faith up until the end:* "You are the Messiah, the Son of the living God" (Mt 16:16). He became the "rock," even if as a man, perhaps, he was nothing more than shifting sand. *Christ Himself is the rock,* and Christ builds His Church on Peter—on Peter, Paul, and the apostles. *The Church is apostolic* in virtue of Christ.

This Church professes: "You are the Messiah, the Son of the living God." Over the centuries this has been the Church's profession of faith, as well as that of those who share her faith and of all those to whom the Father revealed the Son in the Holy Spirit, just as the Son in the Holy Spirit revealed to them the Father (cf. Mt 11:25–27).

This Revelation is *definitive;* one can only accept it or reject it. One can accept it, professing belief in God, the Father Almighty, Creator of heaven and earth, and in Jesus Christ, the Son, of the same substance as the Father and the Holy Spirit, who is Lord and the Giver of life. Or one can reject all of this, writing in capital letters: "God does not have a Son"; "Jesus Christ is not the

Son of God, He is only one of the prophets, and even if not the least of them, he is only a man."

How can we marvel at such arguments when we know that Peter himself had difficulties in this respect? He believed in the Son of God, but he was unable to accept that this Son of God, as a man, could be whipped, crowned with thorns, and then had to die on the Cross.

Is it any wonder that even those who believe in one God, of whom Abraham was a witness, find it difficult to have faith in a crucified God? They hold that God can only be powerful and grandiose, absolutely transcendent and beautiful in His power, holy and inaccessible to man. God can only be this! He cannot be the Father, the Son, and the Holy Spirit. He cannot be Love that gives of Himself and that permits that He be seen, that He be heard, that He be imitated as a man, that He be bound, that He be beaten and crucified. This cannot be God! . . . Therefore, at the center of a great tradition of monotheism a *profound division* was introduced.

In the Church—built on the rock that is Christ—Peter, the apostles, and their successors are witnesses of God crucified and risen in Christ. They are witnesses of the life that is stronger than death. They are witnesses of God who gives life because He is Love (cf. 1 Jn 4:8). They are witnesses because they saw, heard, and touched with their hands the eyes and ears of Peter, John, and many others. But Christ said to Thomas: "Blessed are those who have not seen and have believed" (Jn 20:29).

You rightly assert that *the Pope is a mystery.* You rightly assert that he is a *sign that will be contradicted,* that he is a *challenge.* The old man Simeon said of Christ Himself that He would be "a sign that will be contradicted" (cf. Lk 2:34).

You also contend that, confronted with such a truth—that is, confronted with the Pope—*one must choose;* and for many the choice is not easy. But was it so easy for Peter? Was it easy for any of his successors? Is it easy for the present Pope? To choose requires man's initiative. Christ says: "For flesh and blood has not revealed this to you, but my heavenly Father" (Mt 16:17). This choice, therefore, is not only a human initiative but also an *act of God,* who works and reveals himself through man. And in virtue of such an act of God, a person can repeat, "You are the Messiah, the Son of the living God" (Mt 16:16), and then recite the entire *Creed,* which echoes the profound logic of Revelation. A man can also remind himself, as well as others, of the consequences of this logic of the faith which also display the same *splendor of the truth.* A man can do all of this even though he knows that because of it he will become "a sign that will be contradicted."

What remains for such a man? Only the words that Jesus Himself addressed to the apostles: "If they persecuted me, they will also persecute you. If they kept my word, they will also keep yours" (Jn 15:20). And so: "Have no fear!" *Do not be afraid of God's mystery;* do not be afraid of His love; *and do not be afraid of man's weakness or of his grandeur!* Man does not cease to be great,

not even in his weakness. Do not be afraid of being witnesses to the dignity of every human being, from the
moment of conception until death.

Once again, concerning names: The Pope is called
the "Vicar of Christ." This title should be considered
within the entire context of the Gospel. Before ascend-
ing into heaven, Jesus said to the apostles: "I am with
you always, until the end of the age" (Mt 28:20).
Though invisible, He is personally present in His
Church. He is likewise present in each Christian, by
virtue of baptism and the other sacraments. It was usual
to say, as early as the era of the Fathers, *"Christianus alter
Christus"* ("The Christian is another Christ"), meaning
by this to emphasize *the dignity of the baptized* and his
vocation, through Christ, to holiness.

Furthermore, Christ brings about a special presence
in every priest, who, when celebrating the Eucharist or
administering the sacraments, does so *in persona
Christi*.

From this perspective, the expression "Vicar of
Christ" assumes its true meaning. More than *dignity*, it
alludes to *service*. It emphasizes the duties of the Pope in
the Church, his *Petrine ministry*, carried out for the good
of the Church and the faithful. Saint Gregory the Great
understood this perfectly when, out of all the titles connected to the functions of the Bishop of Rome, he pre-
ferred that of *Servus servorum Dei* (Servant of the
Servants of God).

The Pope is not the only one who holds this title. With regard to the Church entrusted to him, each bishop is *Vicarius Christi*. The Pope is Vicar of Christ with regard to the Church of Rome and, through that Church, of every Church in communion with it—a communion in faith as well as an institutional and canonical communion. Thus, if with this title one wants to refer to the dignity of the Bishop of Rome, one cannot consider it apart from the *dignity of the entire college of bishops,* with which it is tightly bound, as it is to the dignity of each bishop, each priest, and each of the baptized.

What supreme dignity those men and women have who are consecrated, who, as their vocation, have chosen to embrace the nuptial dimension of the Church—Christ's bride! Christ, Redeemer of the world and of humanity, is the Bridegroom of the Church and of all of those who belong to it: "The bridegroom is with them" (cf. Mt 9:15). One duty of the Pope is to profess this truth and to render it present to the Church in Rome as well as to the entire Church, to all humanity, and to the whole world.

To allay to some degree your fears, which seem to arise from a profound faith, I would suggest a reading of Saint Augustine, who often repeated: *"Vobis sum episcopus, vobiscum christianus"* ("I am a bishop for you, I am a Christian with you"; cf., for example, Sermon 340.1: J. P. Migne, ed., *Patrologia Latina* 38.1483). On further reflection, *christianus* has far greater significance than *episcopus,* even if the subject is the Bishop of Rome.

PRAYING: HOW AND WHY

I WOULD LIKE TO TAKE THE LIBERTY TO ASK
you to share with us, at least in part, the secret of
your heart. Given the conviction that within you—as
within every Pope—lives the mystery which is believed
in faith, the following question automatically arises:
How can you bear such a weight, which, in human
terms, is almost unbearable? No man on earth, not even
the highest religious leaders, has a comparable responsibility. No one is placed in such a close relationship
with God.

Your Holiness, how does one address Jesus? How does
one have a dialogue, in prayer, with Christ, who gave
Peter the "keys to the Kingdom of Heaven" (which have
reached you through the apostolic succession), giving
him the power to "bind and loose" all?

YOUR QUESTION CONCERNS PRAYER; YOU ARE asking the Pope *how he prays*. And I thank you. Perhaps it is worth starting with Saint Paul's Letter to the Romans. The apostle comes to the heart of the matter when he writes: *"The Spirit too comes to the aid of our weakness;* for we do not know how to pray as we ought, but the Spirit himself intercedes with inexpressible groanings" (cf. Rom 8:26).

What is prayer? It is commonly held to be a conversation. In a conversation there are always an "I" and a "thou" or "you." In this case the "Thou" is with a capital T. If at first the "I" seems to be the most important element in prayer, prayer teaches that the situation is actually different. *The "Thou" is more important, because our prayer begins with God.* In his Letter to the Romans, Saint Paul teaches precisely this. According to the apostle, prayer reflects all created reality; it is in a certain sense a *cosmic function.*

Man is the priest of all creation; he speaks in its name, but only insofar as he is guided by the Spirit. In order to understand profoundly the meaning of prayer, one should meditate for a long time on the following passage from the Letter to the Romans: "For creation awaits with eager expectation the revelation of the children of God; for creation was made subject to futility, not of its own accord but because of the one who subjected it, in hope that creation itself would be set free from slavery to corruption and share in the glorious freedom of the children of God. We know that all creation is groaning in labor pains even until now; and not only that, but we ourselves, who have the first fruits of the Spirit, we also groan within ourselves as we wait for adoption, the redemption of our bodies. For in hope we were saved" (Rom 8:19–24). And here again we come across the apostle's words: "The Spirit too comes to the aid of our weakness; for we do not know how to pray as we ought, but the Spirit himself intercedes with inexpressible groanings" (cf. Rom 8:26).

In prayer, then, the true protagonist is God. The protagonist is *Christ,* who constantly frees creation from slavery to corruption and leads it toward liberty, for the glory of the children of God. The protagonist is the *Holy Spirit,* who "comes to the aid of our weakness." We begin to pray, believing that it is our own initiative that compels us to do so. Instead, we learn that it is always God's initiative within us, just as Saint Paul has written. *This initiative restores in us our true humanity; it restores in us our unique dignity.* Yes, we are brought into the higher dignity of the children of God, the children of God who are the hope of all creation.

One can and must pray in many different ways, as the Bible teaches through a multitude of examples. *The Book of Psalms is irreplaceable.* We must pray with "inexpressible groanings" in order to enter into *rhythm with the Spirit's own entreaties.* To obtain forgiveness one must implore, becoming part of the loud cries of Christ the Redeemer (cf. Heb 5:7). Through all of this one must proclaim glory. *Prayer is always an opus gloriae* (a work, a labor, of glory). Man is the priest of all creation. Christ conferred upon him this dignity and vocation. Creation completes its *opus gloriae* both by being what it is and by its duty to become what should be.

In a certain sense science and technology also contribute to this goal. But at the same time, since they are human works, they can lead away from this goal. In our civilization in particular there is such a risk, making it difficult for our civilization to be one of life and love. Missing is precisely the *opus gloriae,* which is the fundamental destiny of every creature, and above all *of man, who was created in order to become, in Christ, the priest, prophet, and king of all earthly creatures.*

Much has been written about prayer, and further, prayer has been widely experienced in the history of humankind, especially in the history of Israel and Christianity. Man achieves *the fullness of prayer* not when he expresses himself, but *when he lets God be most fully present in prayer. The history of mystical prayer* in the East and West attests to this: Saint Francis, Saint Teresa of Avila, Saint John of the Cross, Saint Ignatius of Loyola, and, in the East, for example, Saint Serafim of Sarov and many others.

HOW DOES THE POPE PRAY?

FOLLOWING THESE APPROPRIATE AND PRECISE explanations regarding the nature of Christian prayer, I would like to return to the preceding question: How—and for whom, for what—does the Pope pray?

YOU WOULD HAVE TO ASK THE HOLY SPIRIT! The Pope prays *as the Holy Spirit permits him to pray.* I think he has to pray in a way in which, deepening the mystery revealed in Christ, he can better fulfill his ministry. The Holy Spirit certainly guides him in this. But man must not put up obstacles. "The Spirit too comes to help us in our weakness."

For what does the Pope pray? What fills the interior space of his prayer?

The subject of the Pope's prayer is the phrase that begins the last document of the Second Vatican Council, the Pastoral Constitution on the Church in the Modern World: *Gaudium et spes, luctus et angor hominum huius temporis* (The joy and the hope, the grief and the anguish of the people of our time).

Gospel means "good news," and the Good News is always *an invitation to joy.* What is the Gospel? It is a *grand affirmation of the world and of man,* because it is the revelation of the truth about *God. God is the primary source of joy and hope for man.* This is the *God* whom Christ revealed: God who is Creator and Father; God who "so loved the world that he gave his only Son, so that everyone who believes in him might not perish but might have eternal life" (cf. Jn 3:16).

The Gospel, above all else, is *the joy of creation.* God, who in creating saw that His creation was good (cf. Gn 1:1–25), is the source of joy for all creatures, and above all for humankind. God the Creator seems to say of all creation: "It is good that you exist." And His joy spreads especially through the "good news," according to which *good is greater than all that is evil in the world.* Evil, in fact, is neither fundamental nor definitive. This point clearly distinguishes Christianity from all forms of existential pessimism.

Creation was given and entrusted to humankind as a duty, representing not a source of suffering but *the foundation of a creative existence in the world.* A person who believes in the essential goodness of all creation is capable of discovering all the secrets of creation, in order to perfect continually the work assigned to him by God. It must be clear for those who accept Revelation, and in particular the Gospel, that it is better to exist than not to exist. And because of this, in the realm of the Gospel, there is no space for any nirvana, apathy, or resignation. Instead, there is a great challenge to perfect creation— be it oneself, be it the world.

This essential joy of creation is, in turn, completed by the *joy of salvation*, by the *joy of redemption*. The Gospel, above all, is a great joy for the salvation of man. The Creator of man is also his Redeemer. Salvation not only confronts evil in each of its existing forms in this world but proclaims *victory over evil*. "I have conquered the world," says Christ (cf. Jn 16:33). The full promise of these words is found in the Paschal Mystery. During the Easter vigil the Church sings with exultation: *"O felix culpa, quae talem ac tantum meruit habere Redemptorem"* ("Oh happy fault, which gained for us so great a Redeemer!" *Exultet*).

Therefore the cause of our joy is to give us the strength to defeat evil and to embrace the divine filiation which constitutes the essence of the Good News. God gives this power to humankind through Christ. "For God did not send his Son into the world to condemn the world, but that the world might be saved through him" (cf. Jn 3:17).

The work of redemption is to elevate the work of creation to a new level. Creation is permeated with a redemptive sanctification, even a divinization. It comes as if drawn to the sphere of the divinity and of the intimate life of God. In this realm the destructive power of sin is defeated. Indestructible life, revealed in the Resurrection of Christ, "swallows," so to speak, death. "Where, O death, is your victory?" asks the apostle Paul, with his eyes fixed on the Risen Christ (1 Cor 15:55).

Because *the Pope* is a witness of Christ and a minister of the Good News, he is *a man of joy and a man of hope, a man of the fundamental affirmation of the value of existence, the value of creation and of hope in the future life.* Naturally, this is neither a naive joy, nor a vain hope. The joy of the victory over evil does not obfuscate—it actually intensifies—*the realistic awareness of the existence of evil* in the world and in every man. The Gospel teaches us to call good and evil by name, but it also teaches: "Do not be conquered by evil but conquer evil with good" (cf. Rom 12:21).

Here Christian morality is fully expressed. If this morality, however, strives towards values, if it brings a universal affirmation of good, *it can be nothing but extraordinarily demanding.* Good, in fact, is not easy, it is always the "hard road" of which Christ speaks in the Gospel (cf. Mt 7:14). Therefore, *the joy of good and the hope of its triumph* in man and in the world do not exclude *fear for this good, for the disappearance of this hope.*

The Pope, like every Christian, must be keenly *aware of the dangers* to which man is subject in the world, in his temporal future, and in his final, eternal, eschatological future. The awareness of these dangers does not generate pessimism, but rather encourages the struggle for the victory of good in every realm. And it is precisely from this *struggle for the victory of good* in man and in the world *that the need for prayer arises.*

The Pope's prayer, however, has an added dimension. *In his concern for all the churches* every day the Pontiff must open his prayer, his thought, his heart to the entire world. Thus a kind of *geography of the Pope's prayer* is sketched out. It is a geography of communities, churches, societies, and also of the problems that trouble the world today. In this sense the Pope is called to *a universal prayer* in which the *sollicitudo omnium Ecclesiarum* (concern for all the churches; 2 Cor 11:28) permits him to set forth before God all the joys and hopes as well as the griefs and anxieties that the Church shares with humanity today.

Prayer in our time, *prayer in the twentieth century,* should also be discussed. The year 2000 marks a kind of challenge. We must look at the *immensity of good* that has sprung from the mystery of the Incarnation of the Word and, at the same time, not lose sight of the *mystery of sin,* which is continually expanding. Saint Paul writes that "where sin increased" (*"ubi abundavit peccatum"*), "grace overflowed all the more" (*"superabundavit gratia";* cf. Rom 5:20).

This profound truth presents a perennial challenge for prayer. It shows how necessary prayer is for the world and for the Church, because in the end it constitutes *the easiest way of making God and His redeeming love present in the world.* God entrusted to men their own salvation; He entrusted to them the Church and, in the Church, the redeeming work of Christ. God entrusted this to all, both to individuals and to humanity as a whole. *He entrusted all to one and one to all.* The prayer of the Church, and especially the prayer of the Pope, must constantly reflect this awareness.

All of us are "children of the promise" (Gal 4:28). Christ said to the apostles: "Take courage, I have conquered the world" (Jn 16:33). But He also asked: "When the Son of Man comes, will he find faith on earth?" (Lk 18:8). This is the source of *the missionary dimension of the prayer of the Church and of the Pope.*

The Church prays that everywhere the work of salvation will be accomplished through Christ. The Church prays that it can live in constant dedication to God's mission. This mission constitutes, in a certain sense, the essence of the Church, as the Second Vatican Council has stated.

The Church and the Pope pray for the people to whom this mission must be particularly entrusted, they pray for *vocations*—not only for religious and for priestly vocations but also for the many vocations to holiness among God's people amid the laity.

The Church prays for the suffering. Suffering, in fact, is always a great test not only of physical strength but also of spiritual strength. Saint Paul's truth about "completing the sufferings of Christ" (cf. Col 1:24) is part of the Gospel. It contains the joy and the hope that are essential to the Gospel; but man will not cross the threshold of that truth without the help of the Holy Spirit. *Prayer for the suffering and with the suffering is therefore a special part of this great cry* that the Church and the Pope raise together with Christ. It is a cry for the victory of good even through evil, through suffering, through every wrong and human injustice.

The Church *prays for the dead* and this prayer says much about the reality of the Church itself. It says that the Church continues to live in the *hope of eternal life.* Prayer for the dead is almost a battle with the reality of death and destruction that weighs down upon the earthly existence of man. This is and remains a particular *revelation of the Resurrection.* In this prayer Christ Himself bears witness to the life and immortality, to which God calls every human being.

Prayer is a search for God, but it is also *a revelation of God.* Through prayer God reveals Himself as Creator and Father, as Redeemer and Savior, as the Spirit who "scrutinizes everything, even the depths of God" (1 Cor 2:10), and above all "the secrets of human hearts" (cf. Ps 43[44]:22). *Through prayer God reveals Himself above all as Mercy*—that is, Love that goes out to those who are suffering, Love that sustains, uplifts, and invites us to trust. The victory of good in the world is united organically with this truth. A person who prays professes such a truth and in a certain sense makes God, who is *merciful Love,* present in the world.

Does God Really Exist?

The faith of those Catholic Christians, for whom you are shepherd and teacher (in the name of the One Shepherd and Teacher), has three "degrees," three "levels," each linked to the others—God, Jesus Christ, and the Church.

Every Christian believes that *God* exists.

Thus, every Christian believes not only that God has spoken and that He assumed human flesh in a historical figure at the time of the Roman Empire: *Jesus of Nazareth*.

But a Catholic goes beyond this, believing that God and Christ live and act—as in a "body," to use a term from the New Testament—in that *Church*, the visible leader of which, on earth, is the Bishop of Rome.

Faith, certainly, is a gift, a divine grace. But another divine gift is reason. According to the ancient exhortations of the saints and doctors of the Church, the Christian "believes in order to understand"; but he is also called "to understand in order to believe."

Let's start, then, at the beginning. Your Holiness, from a human perspective, can (and how can) one come to the conclusion that God really exists?

Y OUR QUESTION ULTIMATELY CONCERNS *Pascal's distinction* between the Absolute—that is, the *God of the philosophers* (the rationalist *libertins*)—and the *God of Jesus Christ;* and, prior to Him, the God of the Patriarchs—from Abraham to Moses. *Only the God of Jesus Christ is the living God.* As has also been stated in the Dogmatic Constitution on Divine Revelation *Dei Verbum* (no. 3), the first God mentioned above—the God of the philosophers—is the fruit of human thought, of human speculation, and capable of saying something valid about God. In the end, all rationalist arguments follow the path indicated in the Book of Wisdom and the Letter to the Romans—passing from the visible world to the invisible Absolute.

Aristotle and Plato follow this same path, but in a different manner. *The Christian tradition before Thomas Aquinas,* and therefore also Augustine, was tied to Plato, from whom it nonetheless rightfully wanted to distance itself. For Christians, the philosophical Absolute, considered as the First Being or Supreme Good, did not have great meaning. Why engage in philosophical speculations about God, they asked themselves, if the living God has spoken, not only by way of the Prophets but also through His own Son? *The theology of the Fathers,* especially in the East, broke away more and more from Plato and from philosophers in general. Philosophy itself, in the Fathers, ends up in theology (as in the case, for example, in modern times, of Vladimir Soloviev).

Saint Thomas, however, did not abandon the philosophers' approach. He began his *Summa Theologica* with the question *"An Deus sit?"*—"Does God exist?" (cf. 1, q.2, a.3). You ask the same question. This question has proven to be very useful. Not only did it create theodicy, but *this question has reverberated* throughout a highly developed Western civilization. Even if today, unfortunately, the *Summa Theologica* has been somewhat neglected, its initial question persists and continues to resound throughout our civilization.

At this point it is necessary to cite an entire passage from the Pastoral Constitution *Gaudium et Spes* of the Second Vatican Council: "In truth, the imbalances existing in the modern world are linked to a more profound imbalance found in the heart of man. Many elements conflict with each other in man's inner struggle. As a created being, he experiences his limitations in thousands of ways yet he also perceives himself to be boundless in his aspirations and destined to a higher life. Enticed by many options, he is continually forced to choose some and to renounce others. Furthermore, since he is weak and sinful, he often does what he detests and not what he desires. This causes him to suffer an inner division, which is the source of so many and such grievous disagreements in society. . . . With all of this, however, in face of the modern world's development, *there is an ever-increasing number of people who ask themselves or who feel more keenly the most essential questions: What is man? What is the meaning of suffering, of evil, of death, which persist despite all progress? What are these victories, purchased at so high a cost, really worth? What can man offer to society and what can he expect from it? What will there be after this life?* The Church believes that Christ, who died and was resurrected for the sake of all, continuously gives to man through His Spirit the light and the strength to respond to his higher destiny. Nor is there any other name under heaven given to the human race by which we are to be saved. The Church also believes *that the key, the center, and the purpose of all of human history, is found in its Lord and Master"* (*Gaudium et Spes* 10).

This passage of the Council is immensely rich. One clearly sees that *the response to the question "An Deus sit?" is not only an issue that touches the intellect; it is, at the same time, an issue that has a strong impact on all of human existence.* It depends on a multitude of situations in which man searches for the significance and the meaning of his own existence. Questioning God's existence is intimately united *with the purpose of human existence.* Not only is it a question of intellect; it is also a question of the will, even *a question of the human heart* (the *raisons du coeur* of Blaise Pascal). I think that it is wrong to maintain that Saint Thomas's position stands up only in the realm of the rational. One must, it is true, applaud Etienne Gilson when he agrees with Saint Thomas that the intellect is the most marvelous of God's creations, but that does not mean that we must give in to a unilateral rationalism. Saint Thomas celebrates all the richness and complexity of each created being, and especially of the human being. It is not good that his thought has been set aside in the post-conciliar period; he continues, in fact, to be the *master of philosophical and theological universalism*. In this context, his *quinque viae*—that is, his "five ways" that lead toward a response to the question *"An Deus sit?"*—should be read.

"PROOF": IS IT STILL VALID?

ALLOW ME A PARENTHETICAL QUESTION. Clearly one does not challenge the theoretical and philosophical validity of what you have begun to explain. Is this kind of thinking, however, still relevant today for the man who asks himself about God, His existence, His essence?

———

I WOULD SAY, TODAY MORE THAN EVER— certainly more so than in recent times. Essentially, the *positivist mentality,* which developed aggressively between the nineteenth and twentieth centuries, is, in a certain sense, *fading* today. Contemporary man has rediscovered the *sacred,* even if he does not always know how to identify it.

Positivism has not only been a philosophy or a methodology; it has been one of those *schools of suspi-*

cion that the modern era has seen grow and prosper. Is man truly capable of knowing something beyond what he sees with his eyes or hears with his ears? Does some kind of knowledge other than the strictly empirical exist? Is the human capacity for reason completely subject to the senses and internally directed by the laws of mathematics, which have been shown to be particularly useful in the rational ordering of phenomena and for guiding technical progress?

If we put ourselves in the positivist perspective, concepts such as *God or the soul* simply lose meaning. In terms of sensory experience, in fact, nothing corresponds to God or the soul.

In some fields this positivist view is fading. This can be ascertained by comparing the early and the late works of Ludwig Wittgenstein—the Austrian philosopher from the first half of our century.

The fact that human knowledge is primarily a sensory knowledge surprises no one. Neither Plato nor Aristotle nor any of the classical philosophers questioned this. Cognitive realism, both so-called naive realism and critical realism, agrees that *"nihil est in intellectu, quod prius non fuerit in sensu"* ("nothing is in the intellect that was not first in the senses"). Nevertheless, *the limits of these "senses" are not exclusively sensory.* We know, in fact, that man not only knows colors, tones, and forms; he also knows objects *globally*—for example, not only all the parts that comprise the object "man" but also man in himself (yes, man as a person). He knows, therefore, *extrasensory truths,* or, in other words, the *transempirical.* In addition, it is not possible to affirm that when something is transempirical it ceases to be empirical.

It is therefore possible to speak from a solid foundation about *human experience, moral experience, or religious experience.* And if it is possible to speak of such experiences, it is difficult to deny that, in the realm of human experience, one also finds good and evil, truth and beauty, and God. God Himself certainly is not an object of human empiricism; the Sacred Scripture, in its own way, emphasizes this: "No one has ever seen God" (cf. Jn 1:18). If God is a knowable object—as both the Book of Wisdom and the Letter to the Romans teach—He is such on the basis of man's experience both of the visible world and of his interior world. This is the point of departure for Immanuel Kant's study of ethical experience in which he abandons the old approach found in the writings of the Bible and of Saint Thomas Aquinas. Man recognizes himself as an *ethical being,* capable of acting according to criteria of good and evil, and not only those of profit and pleasure. He also recognizes himself as a *religious being,* capable of putting himself in contact with God. Prayer—of which we talked earlier—is in a certain sense the first verification of such a reality.

In gaining some distance from positivistic convictions, contemporary thought has made notable advances toward the ever more complete discovery of man, recognizing among other things the value of metaphorical and symbolic language. Contemporary hermeneutics—examples of which are found in the work of Paul Ricoeur or, from a different perspective, in the work of Emmanuel Lévinas—presents the truth about man and the world from new angles.

Inasmuch as positivism distances us—and, in a certain sense, excludes us—from a more global understanding, hermeneutics, which explores the meaning of symbolic language, permits us to rediscover that more global understanding, and even, in some sense, to deepen it. This is said, obviously, without intending to deny the capacity of reason to form true, conceptual propositions about God and the truths of faith.

For contemporary thought *the philosophy of religion* is very important—for example, the work of Mircea Eliade and, for us in Poland, that of Archbishop Marian Jaworski and the school of Lublin. *We are witnesses of a symptomatic return to metaphysics (the philosophy of being) through an integral anthropology.* One cannot think adequately about man without reference, which for man is constitutive, to God. Saint Thomas defined this as *actus essendi* (essential act), in the language of the *philosophy of existence.* The philosophy of religion expresses this with the categories of *anthropological experience.*

The *philosophers of dialogue,* such as Martin Buber and the aforementioned Lévinas, have contributed greatly to this experience. And we find ourselves by now very close to Saint Thomas, but the path passes not so much through being and existence as through people and their meeting each other, through the "I" and the

"Thou." *This is a fundamental dimension of man's exis-tence, which is always a coexistence.*

Where did the philosophers of dialogue learn this? Foremost, they learned it from their experience of the Bible. In the *sphere of the everyday* man's entire life is one of "coexistence"—"thou" and "I"—and also in the *sphere of the absolute and definitive:* "I" and "THOU." The biblical tradition revolves around this "THOU," who is first the God of Abraham, Isaac, and Jacob, the God of the Fathers, and then the God of Jesus Christ and the apostles, the God of our faith.

Our faith is profoundly anthropological, rooted constitu-tively in coexistence, in the community of God's peo-ple, and *in communion with this eternal "THOU."* Such coexistence is essential to our Judeo-Christian tradition and comes from God's initiative. This initiative is con-nected with and leads to creation, and is at the same time—as Saint Paul teaches—"the eternal election of man in the Word who is the Son" (cf. Eph 1:4).

IF GOD
EXISTS WHY IS
HE HIDING?

GOD, THEN—THE BIBLICAL GOD—EXISTS. BUT isn't the objection of many people, yesterday as today, quite understandable? Why doesn't He reveal Himself more clearly? Why doesn't He give everyone more tangible and accessible proof of His existence? Why does His mysterious strategy seem to be that of playing hide-and-seek with His creatures?

Reasons certainly do exist to believe in Him; but—as many have maintained and still maintain—there are also reasons to doubt, or even deny, His existence. Wouldn't it be simpler if His existence were evident?

THE QUESTIONS YOU ASK—AND WHICH MANY ask—do not refer to Saint Thomas or to Augustine, or to the great Judeo-Christian tradition. It seems to me that they stem from another source, *one that is purely rationalist, one that is characteristic of modern phi-*

losophy—the history of which begins with Descartes, who split thought from existence and identified existence with reason itself: *"Cogito, ergo sum"* ("I think, therefore I am").

How different from the approach of Saint Thomas, for whom it is not *thought which determines existence, but existence, "esse," which determines thought!* I think the way I think because I am that which I am—a creature—and because He is He who is, *the absolute uncreated Mystery.* If He were not Mystery, there would be no need for Revelation, or, more precisely, there would be no need for *God to reveal Himself.*

Your questions would only be legitimate if man, with his created intellect and within the limits of his own subjectivity, could overcome the entire distance that separates creation from the Creator, the contingent and not necessary being from the Necessary Being ("she who is not," according to the well-known words Christ addressed to Saint Catherine of Siena, from "He who is": cf. Raimondo da Capua, *Legenda Maior* 1, 10, 92).

The thoughts that concern you, and which also appear in your books, are expressed by a series of questions. They are not only yours. You wish to be a spokesman for the people of our time, placing yourself at their side on the paths—which are often difficult and intricate, often seeming to lead nowhere—in their search for God. Your anxiety is expressed in your questions: *Why isn't there more concrete proof of God's existence? Why does He seem to hide Himself, almost playing with His creation?*

Shouldn't it all be much simpler? Shouldn't His existence be obvious? These are questions that belong to the repertory of *contemporary agnosticism.* Agnosticism is not atheism; more specifically it is not a systematic atheism, as was Marxist atheism and, in a different context, the atheism of the Enlightenment.

Nevertheless, your questions contain *statements that re-echo the Old and New Testaments.* When you speak of God as hiding, you use almost the same language as Moses, who wanted to see God face to face but could only see his "back" (cf. Ex 33:23). Isn't knowledge through creation suggested here?

When you speak of "playing," I think of words from the Book of Proverbs, which show Wisdom "playing [among the sons of man] on the surface of his earth" (cf. Prv 8:31). Doesn't this mean that the Wisdom of God bestows itself upon all creatures, while at the same time not revealing to them all His Mystery?

God's self-revelation comes about in a special way by his "becoming man." Once again, according to the words of Ludwig Feuerbach, the great temptation is to make the classical reduction of that which is divine to that which is human. It was from Feuerbach's words that Marxist atheism was inspired, but—*ut minus sapiens,* "I am talking like a madman" (cf. 2 Cor 11:23)—*the challenge comes from God Himself,* since He really became man in His Son and was born of the Virgin. It is precisely in this birth, and then through the Passion, the Cross, and the Resurrection that the self-revelation of God in the history of man reached its zenith—the revelation of the invisible God in the visible humanity of Christ.

Even the day before the Passion the apostles asked Christ: "Show us the Father" (Jn 14:8). His response remains fundamental: "How can you say, 'Show us the Father'? Do you not believe that I am in the Father and the Father is in me? . . . Or else, believe because of the works themselves. . . . The Father and I are one" (cf. Jn 14:9–11; 10:30).

Christ's words are far-reaching. We are almost at the point of *that direct experience* to which contemporary man aspires. But this immediacy is not the knowledge of God "face to face" (1 Cor 13:12), the knowledge of God as God.

Let's try to be impartial in our reasoning: *Could God go further in His stooping down, in His drawing near to man,* thereby expanding the possibilities of our knowing Him? In truth, *it seems that He has gone as far as possible. He could not go further.* In a certain sense God has gone too far! Didn't Christ perhaps become "a stumbling block to Jews and foolishness to Gentiles" (1 Cor 1:23)? Precisely because He called God His Father, because He revealed Him so openly in Himself, He could not but elicit the impression that it was too much. . . . Man was no longer able to tolerate such closeness, and thus the protests began.

This great protest has precise names—first it is called the Synagogue, and then Islam. Neither can accept a God who is so human. "It is not suitable to speak of God in this way," they protest. "He must remain absolutely transcendent; He must remain pure Majesty. Majesty full of mercy, certainly, but not to the point of paying for the faults of His own creatures, for their sins."

From one point of view it is right to say that God revealed too much of Himself to man, too much of that which is most divine, that which is His intimate life; He revealed Himself in His Mystery. He was not mindful of the fact that such an *unveiling would in a certain way obscure Him in the eyes of man, because man is not capable of withstanding an excess of the Mystery.* He does not want to be pervaded and overwhelmed by it. Yes, man knows that God is the One in whom "we live and move and have our being" (Acts 17:28); but why must that be confirmed by His Death and Resurrection? Yet Saint Paul writes: "If Christ has not been raised, then empty is our preaching; empty, too, your faith" (1 Cor 15:14).

IS JESUS THE SON OF GOD?

FROM THE "PROBLEM" OF GOD, LET'S MOVE ON to the "problem" of Jesus, as in fact you have already begun to do.

Why isn't Jesus simply considered a wise man like Socrates? Or a prophet like Muhammad? Or enlightened like Buddha? How does one maintain the unprecedented certainty that this Jew condemned to death in an obscure province is the Son of God, of one being with the Father? This radical Christian claim has no parallel in any other religious belief. Saint Paul himself defined it as "a scandal and madness."

SAINT PAUL IS PROFOUNDLY AWARE THAT *Christ is absolutely original and absolutely unique.* If He were only a wise man like Socrates, if He were a "prophet" like Muhammad, if He were "enlightened" like Buddha, without any doubt He would not be what He is. He is *the one mediator between God and humanity.*

He is mediator because He is both God and man. He holds within Himself the entire intimate world of divinity, the entire Mystery of the Trinity, and the mystery both of temporal life and of immortality. He is true man. In Him the divine is not confused with the human. There remains something essentially divine.

But at the same time Christ is so human! Thanks to this, *the entire world of men, the entire history of humanity, finds in Him its expression before God.* And not before a distant, unreachable God, but before a God that is in Him—that indeed is He. This is not found in any other religion, much less in any philosophy.

Christ is unique! Unlike *Muhammad,* He does more than just promulgate principles of religious discipline to which all God's worshipers must conform. Christ is not simply a wise man as was *Socrates,* whose free acceptance of death in the name of truth nevertheless has a similarity with the sacrifice of the Cross.

Less still is He similar to *Buddha,* with his denial of all that is created. Buddha is right when he does not see the possibility of human salvation in creation, but he is wrong when, for that reason, he denies that creation has any value for humanity. Christ does not do this, nor can He do this. *He is the eternal witness to the Father and to the love that the Father has had for His creatures from the beginning.* The Creator, from the beginning, saw a multitude of good in creation; He saw it especially in man, made in His image and likeness. He saw this good in His incarnate Son. He saw it as a duty for His Son and for all rational creatures. Pushing the divine vision to the limits, we can say that God saw this good specifically in the Passion and in the Death of His Son.

This good would be confirmed at the Resurrection, which is the beginning of a new creation, the rediscovery of all creation in God, of the final destiny of all creatures. And this destiny is expressed in the fact that God will be "all in all" (1 Cor 15:28).

From the beginning Christ has been at the center of the faith and life of the Church, and also at the center of her teaching and theology. As for her teaching, it is necessary to go back to the entire first millennium, from the First Council of Nicaea to those of Ephesus and Chalcedon, and then finally to the Second Council of Nicaea, which evolved out of the Councils that preceded it. All of the Councils from the first millennium revolve around the Mystery of the Holy Trinity, including the procession of the Holy Spirit, but *at their roots, all are Christological.* From the time Peter confessed, "You are the Messiah, the Son of the living God" (Mt 16:16), Christ has been at the center of the faith and life of Christians, at the center of their witness, which often led to the shedding of their blood.

Thanks to this faith and in spite of the persecutions, the Church experienced a continual expansion. The faith progressively christianized the ancient world. Following the confession of Peter at Caesarea Philippi, true faith in Christ, God and man, did not cease to be the center of the Church's life, witness, worship, and liturgy, even when the threat of Arianism later emerged. *It could be said that from the very beginning there was a Christological focus in Christianity.*

Above all, this is true of the faith and the living tradition of the Church. A remarkable expression of it is found in Marian devotion and in Mariology: "He was conceived by the Holy Spirit and born of the Virgin Mary" (Apostles' Creed). *A Marian dimension and Mariology in the Church are simply another aspect of the Christological focus.*

One must never tire of repeating this. Despite some common aspects, Christ does not resemble Muhammad or Socrates or Buddha. *He is totally original and unique.* The uniqueness of Christ, as indicated by Peter's words at Caesarea Philippi, is the center of the Church's faith, as expressed by the Creed: *"I believe* in God, the Father Almighty, Creator of heaven and earth; and *in Jesus Christ, His only Son, our Lord, who was conceived by the Holy Spirit, born of the Virgin Mary,* suffered under Pontius Pilate, was crucified, died, and was buried. He descended into hell; the third day He rose again from the dead; He ascended into heaven, and sits at the right hand of God the Father Almighty."

This so-called Apostles' Creed is the expression of the faith of Peter and of the whole Church. Then, beginning in the fourth century the *Nicene-Constantinopolitan*

Creed entered into catechetical and liturgical use, enriching her teaching. It enriched that teaching thanks to the increased awareness which the Church gained as she progressively entered into Greek culture and more clearly realized the need for ways of presenting her doctrine which would be adequate and convincing in that cultural context.

At Nicaea and Constantinople it was affirmed that Jesus Christ was "the Only-begotten Son of God. Born of the Father before all ages. . . . Begotten, not made, of one being with the Father; by Whom all things were made" (Nicene Creed).

These formulations are not simply the fruit of Greek culture; *they come directly from the apostolic heritage.* If we want to look for the *source* of these ideas, we will find it *first of all in Paul and John.*

Paul's Christology is extraordinarily rich. His starting point is an event that occurred at the gates of Damascus. The young Pharisee was blinded, but at the same time, with the eyes of his soul he saw the whole truth about the Risen Christ. He then expressed this truth in his Letters.

The words of the Nicene Creed are nothing other than the reflection of Paul's doctrine. These words also contain the heritage of John, particularly (but not only) in the Prologue of his Gospel (cf. Jn 1:1–18). His whole Gospel, as well as his Letters, are a witness to the Word of Life, to "what we have heard, / what we have seen

with our own eyes, / . . . and touched with our hands"
(1 Jn 1:1).

In a certain respect, John has greater qualifications as a
witness than does Paul, even if Paul's testimony is so
deeply moving. *This comparison between Paul and John is*
important. John wrote after Paul. Therefore, it is above
all in the writing of Paul that one must search for the
first expressions of the faith.

And not only in Paul, but *also in Luke,* who was a fol-
lower of Paul. In fact, in Luke there is a passage that
could be considered a *bridge between Paul and John.* I am
referring to the words uttered by Christ and recorded by
Luke—"he rejoiced in the Holy Spirit" (cf. Lk 10:21): "I
give you praise, Father, Lord of heaven and earth, for
although you have hidden these things from the wise
and the learned you have revealed them to the child-
like. . . . No one knows who the Son is except the
Father, and who the Father is except the Son and anyone
to whom the Son wishes to reveal him" (Lk 10:21–22).
Here Luke expresses precisely what Matthew quotes
Jesus as saying to Peter: "For flesh and blood has not
revealed this to you, but my heavenly Father" (Mt 16:17).
There is an exact relationship between Luke's affirmation and John's words in his Prologue: "No one has ever
seen God. The only Son, God, who is at the Father's
side, has revealed him" (Jn 1:18).

This Gospel truth reappears many times in the writings of John. *The Christology of the New Testament is*
"explosive." The Fathers, the great Scholastics, the the-

ologians of the ensuing centuries *did nothing other than return, always with renewed wonder, to the heritage they had received,* in order to grow in a deeper understanding of it.

You will remember that my first encyclical on the Redeemer of man (*Redemptor Hominis*) appeared a few months after my election on October 16, 1978. This means that I was actually carrying its contents *within me.* I had only to "copy" from memory and experience what I had already been living on the threshold of the papacy.

I emphasize this because the encyclical represents a confirmation, on the one hand, of the *tradition of the schools* from which I came and, on the other hand, of the *pastoral style,* reflected in this encyclical. The Council proposed, especially in *Gaudium et Spes,* that the mystery of redemption should be seen in light of the great renewal of man and of all that is human. The encyclical aims to be *a great hymn of joy for the fact that man has been redeemed through Christ*—redeemed in spirit and in body. This redemption of the body subsequently found its own expression in the series of catecheses for the Wednesday Papal audiences: *"Male and female He created them."* Perhaps it would be better to say: "Male and female He redeemed them."

What Has Become of the "History of Salvation"?

Taking advantage of the freedom you have granted me, I will continue to ask questions that might, perhaps, seem strange to you. As you have observed, however, they are questions asked by many of our contemporaries, who, confronted with the message of the Gospel which the Church continues to proclaim, ask themselves: Why does the "history of salvation" (as Christians refer to it) appear so complicated? In order to pardon us and to save us, did a God who is a loving Father really need to sacrifice cruelly His own Son?

Your question, concerning the *history of salvation,* touches upon the most profound significance of redemptive salvation. Let's begin by looking at *the history of European thought after Descartes.* I put Descartes in the forefront because he marks the beginning of a new era in the history of European thought and because this philosopher, who is certainly among the greatest that France has given the world, inaugurated the *great anthropocentric shift in philosophy.* "I think, therefore I am," as previously mentioned, is the motto of modern rationalism.

All the rationalism of the last centuries—as much in its Anglo-Saxon expression as in its Continental expression in Kantianism, Hegelianism, and the German philosophy of the nineteenth and twentieth centuries up to Husserl and Heidegger—can be considered a continuation and an expansion of Cartesian positions. The author of *Meditationes de Prima Philosophia* with his ontological proofs, *distanced us from the philosophy of existence,* and also from the traditional approaches of Saint Thomas which lead to God who is "autonomous existence," *Ipsum esse subsistens.* By making subjective consciousness absolute, Descartes moves instead toward *pure consciousness of the Absolute,* which is *pure thought.* Such an Absolute is not *autonomous existence,* but rather *autonomous thought.* Only that which corresponds to human thought makes sense. The objective truth of this thought is not as important as the fact that something exists in human consciousness.

We find ourselves on the threshold of *modern immanentism* and *subjectivism.* Descartes marks the beginning of the development of the exact and natural sciences as well as of the humanistic sciences in their new expression. He turns his back on metaphysics and concentrates on the philosophy of knowledge. Kant is the most notable representative of this movement.

. . .

Though the father of modern rationalism certainly cannot be blamed for the move away from Christianity, it is difficult not to acknowledge that he created the climate in which, in the modern era, such an estrangement became possible. It did not happen right away, but gradually.

In fact, about 150 years after Descartes, all that was *fundamentally Christian* in the tradition of European thought *had already been pushed aside.* This was the time of the Enlightenment in France, when *pure rationalism held sway.* The French Revolution, during the Reign of Terror, knocked down the altars dedicated to Christ, tossed crucifixes into the streets, introduced the cult of the goddess Reason. On the basis of this, there was a proclamation of *Liberty, Equality, and Fraternity.* The spiritual patrimony and, in particular, the moral patrimony of Christianity were thus torn from their evangelical foundation. In order to restore Christianity to its full vitality, it is essential that these return to that foundation.

Nevertheless, the process of turning away from the God of the Fathers, from the God of Jesus Christ, from the Gospel, and from the Eucharist did not bring about a rupture with a God who exists outside of the world. In fact, *the God of the deists was always present;* perhaps He was even present in the French Encyclopedists, in the work of Voltaire and of Jean-Jacques Rousseau, and even more so in Isaac Newton's *Philosophiae Naturalis Principia Mathematica,* which marked the beginning of modern physics.

. . .

This God, however, is decidedly *a God outside of the world*. To a mentality shaped by a naturalistic consciousness of the world, a God present in the world appeared useless; similarly, a God working through man turned out to be useless to modern knowledge, to the modern science of man, which examines the workings of the conscious and the subconscious. *The rationalism of the Enlightenment put to one side the true God—in particular, God the Redeemer.*

The consequence was that *man was supposed to live by his reason alone, as if God did not exist.* Not only was it necessary to leave God out of the objective knowledge of the world, since the existence of a Creator or of Providence was in no way helpful to science, it was also necessary to act as if God did not exist, as if God were not interested in the world. *The rationalism of the Enlightenment was able to accept a God outside of the world primarily because it was an unverifiable hypothesis. It was crucial, however, that such a God be expelled from the world.*

THE CENTRALITY OF
SALVATION

I AM FOLLOWING YOUR PHILOSOPHICAL ARGU-
ment with keen attention. But how does this tie
in with the question I asked about the "history of salvation"?

T HAT IS PRECISELY WHAT I INTEND TO GET TO.
With such a way of thinking and acting, the rationalism of the Enlightenment strikes at the heart of
Christian soteriology, that is, theological reflection on salvation (*sōtēria,* in Greek) and of redemption. "God so
loved the world that he gave his only Son, so that everyone who believes in him might not perish but might
have eternal life" (Jn 3:16). In this conversation with
Nicodemus every word of Christ's response constitutes
a point of contention for a *forma mentis* (mind-set) born
of the Enlightenment—not only the French Enlightenment but the English and German as well.

. . .

Addressing the question "Why is the history of salvation so complicated?"—a question which resonates for many today—let us analyze the words of Christ in the Gospel of John in order to understand where we find ourselves at odds with this *forma mentis.*

Actually, it is *very simple!* We can easily demonstrate its profound simplicity and wonderful internal logic by starting with the words Jesus addressed to Nicodemus.

The first affirmation is: *"God so loved the world."* According to the Enlightenment mentality, the world does not need God's love. *The world is self-sufficient.* And God, in turn, is not, above all, Love. If anything, He is Intellect, an intellect that eternally knows. No one needs His intervention in the world that exists, that is self-sufficient, that is transparent to human knowledge, that is ever more free of mysteries thanks to scientific research, that is ever more an inexhaustible mine of raw materials for man—*the demi-god* of modern technology. *This is the world that must make man happy.*

Christ instead says to Nicodemus: "God so loved the world that he gave his only Son, so that everyone who believes in him might not perish" (cf. Jn 3:16). In this way Jesus makes us understand that the world is not the source of man's ultimate happiness. Rather, it can become the source of his ruin. This world which appears to be a great workshop in which knowledge is developed by man, which appears as progress and civilization, as a modern system of communications, as a structure of democratic freedoms without any limitations, this world is not capable of making men happy.

When Christ speaks of the love that the Father has for the world, He merely echoes the first affirmation in the Book of Genesis which accompanies the description of creation: "God saw how good it was. . . . He found it very good" (Gn 1:12–31). But this affirmation in no way constitutes the *absolute assurance of salvation*. The world is not capable of making man happy. It is not capable of saving him from evil, in all of its types and forms—illness, epidemics, cataclysms, catastrophes, and the like. This world, with its riches and its wants, needs to be saved, to be redeemed.

The world is not able to free man from suffering; specifically it is not able to free him from death. *The entire world is subject to "precariousness,"* as Saint Paul says in the Letter to the Romans; it is subject to corruption and mortality. Insofar as his body is concerned, so is man. Immortality is not a part of this world. It can come to man exclusively from God. This is why Christ speaks of God's love that expresses itself in the offering of His only Son, so that man "might not perish but might have eternal life" (Jn 3:16). *Eternal life can be given to man only by God; it can be only His gift.* It cannot be given to man by the created world. Creation—and man together with it—is subject to "futility" (cf. Rom 8:20).

. . .

"God did not send his Son into the world to condemn the world, but that the world might be saved through him" (cf. Jn 3:17). The world that the Son of man found when He became man deserved condemnation, *because of the sin* that had dominated all of history, beginning with the fall of our first parents. This is another point that is absolutely unacceptable to post-Enlightenment thought. *It refuses to accept the reality of sin and, in particular, it refuses to accept original sin.*

When, during my last visit to Poland, I chose the Decalogue and the commandment of love as a theme for the homilies, all the Polish followers of the "enlightened agenda" were upset. For such people, the Pope becomes *persona non grata* when he tries to convince the world of human sin. Objections of this sort conflict with that which Saint John expresses in the words of Christ, who announced the coming of the Holy Spirit who *"will convince the world in regard to sin"* (cf. Jn 16:8). What else can the Church do? Nevertheless, convincing the world of the existence of sin is not the same as condemning it for sinning. "God did not send his Son into the world to condemn the world, but that the world might be saved through him." *Convincing the world of sin means creating the conditions for its salvation.* Awareness of our own sinfulness, including that which is inherited, is the first condition for salvation; the next is the confession of this sin before God, who desires only to receive this confession so that He can save man. *To save means to embrace and lift up with redemptive love,* with love that is *always greater* than any sin. In this regard the parable of the prodigal son is an unsurpassable paradigm.

The history of salvation is *very simple.* And it is a history that unfolds within the earthly history of humanity, beginning with the first Adam, through the revelation of the second Adam, Jesus Christ (cf. 1 Cor 15:45), and ending with the ultimate fulfillment of the history of the world in God, when He will be "all in all" (1 Cor 15:28).

At the same time, this history *embraces the life of every man.* In a certain sense it is entirely contained in the parable of the prodigal son, or in the words of Christ when He addresses the adulteress: "Neither do I condemn you. Go, [and] from now on do not sin anymore" (Jn 8:11).

The history of salvation is synthesized in the fundamental observation of God's great intervention in the history of humankind. This intervention reaches its culmination in the Paschal Mystery—the Passion, Death, Resurrection, and Ascension of Christ to heaven—and is completed at Pentecost, with the descent of the Holy Spirit upon the apostles. This history, while it reveals the redemptive will of God, also reveals *the mission of the Church.* It is the history of every individual and the entire human family, created in the beginning and then re-created in Christ and in the Church. Saint Augustine had a profound insight into this history when he wrote *De Civitate Dei (The City of God).* But he was not the only one.

. . .

The history of salvation continues to offer new inspiration for interpreting the history of humanity. Because of this, numerous contemporary thinkers and historians are also interested in the history of salvation. It is, in fact, the most stimulating of themes. All of the questions raised by the Second Vatican Council are reducible, finally, to this theme.

The history of salvation not only addresses the question of human history but also confronts *the problem of the meaning of man's existence.* As a result, it is both *history* and *metaphysics.* It could be said that it is the *most integral* form of theology, the theology of all the encounters between God and the world. The Pastoral Constitution on the Church in the Modern World, *Gaudium et Spes,* is nothing other than a contemporary presentation of this great theme.

WHY IS THERE
SO MUCH EVIL
IN THE WORLD?

Y OUR WORDS OPEN UP FOR US GRAND AND
fascinating prospects that, for believers, are certainly further confirmations of their hope.

And yet, we cannot forget that in every century, at the
hour of truth, even Christians have asked themselves a
tormenting question: How to continue to trust in a God
who is supposed to be a merciful Father, in a God who—
as the New Testament reveals—is meant to be Love itself,
when suffering, injustice, sickness, and death seem to
dominate the larger history of the world as well as our
smaller daily lives?

S TAT CRUX DUM VOLVITUR ORBIS (THE CROSS
remains constant while the world turns). As I stated
earlier, we find ourselves at the center of the history of
salvation. Naturally you could not fail to bring up that

which is *the source of recurring doubt* not only in regard to the goodness of God but also in regard to His very existence. How could God have permitted so many wars, concentration camps, the Holocaust?

Is the God who allows all this still truly Love, as Saint John proclaims in his First Letter? Indeed, is He just with respect to His creatures? Doesn't He place too many burdens on the shoulders of individuals? Doesn't He leave man alone with these burdens, condemning him to a life without hope? So many incurably ill people in hospitals, so many handicapped children, so many human lives completely denied ordinary happiness on this earth, the happiness that comes from love, marriage, and family. All this adds up to a bleak picture, which has found expression in ancient and modern literature. Consider, for example, Fyodor Dostoyevsky, Franz Kafka, or Albert Camus.

God created man as rational and free, thereby placing Himself under man's judgment. *The history of salvation is also the history of man's continual judgment of God.* Not only of man's questions and doubts but of his actual judgment of God. In part, the Old Testament Book of Job is the paradigm of this judgment. There is also the intervention of the evil spirit, who, with even greater shrewdness than man, would judge not only man but God's actions in human history. This too is confirmed in the Book of Job.

. . .

Scandalum Crucis (The Scandal of the Cross). In the preceding questions you addressed the problem precisely: Was putting His Son to death on the Cross necessary for the salvation of humanity?

Given our present discussion, we must ask ourselves: Could it have been different? Could God have *justified Himself* before human history, so full of suffering, without placing Christ's Cross at the center of that history? Obviously, one response could be that God does not need to justify Himself to man. It is enough that He is omnipotent. From this perspective everything He does or allows must be accepted. This is the position of the biblical Job. But God, who besides being Omnipotence is Wisdom and—to repeat once again—Love, desires to justify Himself to mankind. He is not the Absolute that remains outside of the world, indifferent to human suffering. He is Emmanuel, God-with-us, a God who shares man's lot and participates in his destiny. This brings to light another inadequacy, the completely false image of God which the Enlightenment accepted uncritically. With regard to the Gospel, this image certainly represented a step backward, not in the direction of a better knowledge of God and the world, but in the direction of misunderstanding them.

No, absolutely not! God is not someone who remains only outside of the world, content to be in Himself all-knowing and omnipotent. *His wisdom and omnipotence are placed, by free choice, at the service of creation.* If suffering is present in the history of humanity, one understands why His omnipotence was manifested *in the omnipotence of humiliation on the Cross.* The scandal of the Cross remains the key to the interpretation of the great mystery of suffering, which is so much a part of the history of mankind.

Even contemporary critics of Christianity are in agreement on this point. Even they see that the crucified Christ is *proof of God's solidarity with man in his suffering.* God places Himself on the side of man. He does so in a radical way: "He emptied himself, / taking the form of a slave, / coming in human likeness; / and found human in appearance, / he humbled himself, / becoming obedient to death, / even death on a cross" (Phil 2:7–8). Everything is contained in this statement. All individual and collective suffering caused by the forces of nature and unleashed by man's free will—the wars, the gulags, and the holocausts: the Holocaust of the Jews but also, for example, the holocaust of the black slaves from Africa.

Why Does
God Tolerate
Suffering?

T HE OBJECTION OF MANY PEOPLE TO THE previous response is well known—the question of pain and evil in the world is not really faced but only displaced. Faith affirms that God is omnipotent. Why, then, hasn't He eliminated—and does He persist in not eliminating—suffering in the world He created? Aren't we being presented with a sort of "divine impotence," the kind spoken of even by people who are sincerely religious, though perhaps deeply troubled in their faith?

Y ES, IN A CERTAIN SENSE ONE COULD SAY that *confronted with our human freedom, God decided to make Himself "impotent."* And one could say that God is paying for the great gift bestowed upon a being He created "in his image, after his likeness" (cf. Gn 1:26). Before this gift, He remains consistent, and *places Himself before the judgment of man,* before an illegitimate tri-

bunal which asks Him provocative questions: "Then
you are a king?" (cf. Jn 18:37); "Is it true that all which
happens in the world, in the history of Israel, in the history of all nations, depends on you?"

We know Christ's response to this question before
Pilate's tribunal: "For this I was born and for this I came
into the world, to testify to the truth" (Jn 18:37). But
then: "What is truth?" (Jn 18:38), and here ended the
judicial proceeding, that tragic proceeding in which
man accused God before the tribunal of his own history, and in which the sentence handed down did not
conform to the truth. Pilate says: "I find no guilt in
him" (Jn 18:38), and a second later he orders: "Take him
yourselves and crucify him!" (Jn 19:6). In this way he
washes his hands of the issue and returns the responsibility to the violent crowd.

Therefore, *the condemnation of God by man is not based
on the truth, but on arrogance, on an underhanded conspir-
acy.* Isn't this the truth about the history of humanity,
the truth about our century? In our time the same condemnation has been repeated in many courts of oppressive totalitarian regimes. And isn't it also being repeated
in the parliaments of democracies where, for example,
laws are regularly passed condemning to death a person
not yet born?

God is always on the side of the suffering. His omnipotence is manifested precisely in the fact that He freely
accepted suffering. He could have chosen not to do so.
He could have chosen to demonstrate His omnipotence

even at the moment of the Crucifixion. In fact, it was proposed to Him: "Let the Messiah, the King of Israel, come down now from the cross that we may see and believe" (Mk 15:32). But He did not accept that challenge. The fact that He stayed on the Cross until the end, the fact that on the Cross He could say, as do all who suffer: "My God, my God, why have you forsaken me?" (Mk 15:34), has remained in human history *the strongest argument*. If the agony on the Cross had not happened, the truth that God is Love would have been unfounded.

Yes! God is Love and precisely for this He gave His Son, to reveal Himself completely as Love. Christ is the One who *"loved . . . to the end"* (Jn 13:1). "To the end" means to the last breath. "To the end" means accepting all the consequences of man's sin, taking it upon Himself. This happened exactly as prophet Isaiah affirmed: "It was our infirmities that he bore, / . . . We had all gone astray like sheep, / each following his own way; / But the Lord laid upon him / the guilt of us all" (Is 53:4–6).

The Man of Suffering is the revelation of that Love which "endures all things" (1 Cor 13:7), of that Love which is the "greatest" (cf. 1 Cor 13:13). It is the revelation not only that God is Love but also the One who "pours out love into our hearts through the Holy Spirit" (cf. Rom 5:5). In the end, before Christ Crucified, the man who shares in redemption will have the advantage over the man who sets himself up as an unbending judge of God's actions in his own life as well as in that of all humanity.

. . .

Thus we find ourselves *at the center of the history of salvation.* The judgment of God becomes a judgment of man. The divine realm and the human realm of this event meet, cross, and overlap. Here we must stop. From the Mount of the Beatitudes, the road of the Good News leads to Calvary, and passes through Mount Tabor, the Mount of the Transfiguration. The difficulty and the challenge of understanding the meaning of Calvary is so great that God Himself wanted to warn the apostles of all that would have to happen between Good Friday and Easter Sunday.

This is the definitive meaning of Good Friday: *Man, you who judge God,* who order Him to justify Himself before your tribunal, think about yourself, if you are not responsible for the death of this condemned man, *if the judgment of God is not actually a judgment upon yourself.* Consider if this judgment and its result—the Cross and then the Resurrection—are not your only way to salvation.

When the archangel Gabriel announced to the Virgin of Nazareth the birth of the Son, revealing that His Reign would be unending (cf. Lk 1:33), it was certainly difficult to foresee that those words augured such a future; that the Reign of God in the world would come about at such a cost; that from that moment on the history of the salvation of all humanity would have to follow such a path.

Only from that moment? Or also from the very beginning? The event at Calvary is a historical fact.

Nevertheless, it is not limited in time and space. It goes back into the past, to the beginning, and opens toward the future until the end of history. It encompasses all places and times and all of mankind. Christ is *the expectation* and simultaneously *the fulfillment*. "There is no salvation through anyone else, nor is there any other name under heaven given to the human race by which we are to be saved" (Acts 4:12).

Christianity is a religion of salvation—a soteriological religion, to use the theological term. Christian soteriology focuses on the Paschal Mystery. In order to hope for salvation from God, man must stop beneath Christ's Cross. Then, the Sunday after the Holy Sabbath, he must stand in front of the empty tomb and listen, like the women of Jerusalem: "He is not here, for he has been raised" (Mt 28:6). Contained within the Cross and the Resurrection is the certainty that God saves man, that He saves him through Christ, through His Cross and His Resurrection.

WHAT DOES "TO SAVE" MEAN?

THE HOLY FATHER IS AWARE OF THE FACT that in today's culture we "common people" risk losing an understanding of the deepest meaning of the Christian vision.

I ask you, then, in concrete terms, for faith, what does it mean "to save"? What is this "salvation" which, as you say, is at the heart of Christianity?

TO SAVE MEANS TO LIBERATE FROM EVIL. This does not refer only to social evils, such as injustice, coercion, exploitation. Nor does it refer only to disease, catastrophes, natural cataclysms, and everything that has been considered disaster in the history of humanity.

To save means to liberate from *radical, ultimate evil.* Death itself is no longer that kind of evil, if followed by the Resurrection. And the Resurrection comes about through the work of Christ. *Through the work of the Redeemer death ceases to be an ultimate evil; it becomes subject to the power of life.*

The world does not have such power. The world, which is capable of perfecting therapeutic techniques in various fields, does not have the power to liberate man from death. And therefore the world cannot be a source of salvation for man. *Only God saves,* and He saves the whole of humanity in Christ. *The very name Jesus, Jeshua ("God who saves"),* bespeaks this salvation. In the course of history, many Israelites had this name, but it can be said that this name was waiting for this Son of Israel alone, who was meant to confirm its truth: "Was it not I, the Lord, besides whom there is no other God? There is no just and saving God but me" (cf. Is 45:21).

To save means *to liberate from radical evil.* This evil is not only man's progressive decline with the passage of time and his final engulfment in the abyss of death. An even more radical evil is God's rejection of man, that is, *eternal damnation* as the consequence of man's rejection of God.

Damnation is the opposite of salvation. Both are associated with the destiny of man to live eternally. Both presuppose the immortality of the human being. Temporal death cannot destroy man's destiny of eternal life.

And what is this eternal life? It is happiness that comes from *union with God.* Christ affirms: "Now this is eternal life, that they should know you, the only true God, and the one whom you sent, Jesus Christ" (Jn 17:3). Union with God is realized in the vision of the Divine Being "face to face" (1 Cor 13:12), a vision called "beatific" because it carries with it the ultimate attainment of man's aspiration to truth. In place of the many partial truths which man arrives at through prescientific and scientific knowledge, the vision of God "face to face" allows enjoyment of the *absolute fullness of truth*. In this way man's aspiration to truth is ultimately satisfied.

Salvation, however, is not reducible to this. In knowing God "face to face," man encounters *the absolute fullness of good*. The platonic intuition of the idea of good found in Christianity its ultraphilosophical and ultimate confirmation. What we are speaking of here is not union with the idea of good, but rather union with Good itself. God is this Good. To the young man who asked, "Good teacher, what must I do to inherit eternal life?" Christ responded: "Why do you call me good? No one is good but God alone" (Mk 10:17–18).

As the fullness of Good, *God is the fullness of life.* Life is in Him and from Him. This is life that has no limits in time or space. It is "eternal life," participation in the life of God Himself, which comes about in the eternal communion of the Father, the Son, and the Holy Spirit. The dogma of the Holy Trinity expresses the truth about the intimate life of God and invites us to receive that life. In Jesus Christ man is called to such a participation and led toward it.

Eternal life is exactly this. The Death of Christ gives life, because it allows believers to share in His Resurrection. The Resurrection is the revelation of life, which is affirmed as present beyond the boundary of death. Before His own Death and Resurrection, Christ raised Lazarus, but before doing so He had a meaningful conversation with Lazarus's sisters. Martha says: "Lord, if you had been here, my brother would not have died." Christ: "Your brother will rise." Martha replies: "I know he will rise, in the resurrection on the last day." And Jesus answers: "I am the resurrection and the life; whoever believes in me, even if he dies, will live, and everyone who lives and believes in me will never die" (Jn 11:21, 23–26).

These words spoken on the occasion of the resurrection of Lazarus contain the truth about the resurrection of the body through Christ. His Resurrection, His victory over death, embraces every man. We are called to salvation, we are called to participate in life, which has been revealed through the Resurrection of Christ.

According to Saint Matthew, this resurrection of the body is to be preceded by a *judgment* passed upon the works of charity, fulfilled or neglected. As a result of this *judgment,* the just are destined to eternal life. There is a destination to eternal damnation as well, which consists in the ultimate rejection of God, the ultimate break of the communion with the Father and the Son and the Holy Spirit. *Here, it is not so much God who rejects man, but man who rejects God.*

Eternal damnation is certainly proclaimed in the Gospel. To what degree is it realized in life beyond the grave? This is, ultimately, a great mystery. However, we can never forget that God "wills everyone to be saved and to come to knowledge of the truth" (1 Tm 2:4).

Happiness springs from the knowledge of the truth, from the vision of God face to face, from sharing in His life. This happiness is so profoundly a part of man's deepest aspiration that the words just cited above from the first letter to Timothy seem fully justified: the One who has created man with this fundamental desire cannot behave differently from what the revealed text indicates; He cannot but want "everyone to be saved and to come to knowledge of the truth."

Christianity is a religion of salvation. The salvation in question is that of the Cross and the Resurrection. God, who desires that man "may live" (cf. Ez 18:23), draws near to him through the death of His Son in order to reveal that life to which he is called in God Himself. Everyone who looks for salvation, not only the Christian, must stop before the Cross of Christ.

Will he be willing to accept the truth of the Paschal Mystery, or not? Will he have faith? This is yet another issue. *This Mystery of salvation is an event which has already taken place.* God has embraced all men by the Cross and the Resurrection of His Son. God embraces all men with the life which was revealed in the Cross and in the Resurrection, and which is constantly being born anew from them. As indicated by the allegory of "the vine" and "the branches" in the Gospel of John (cf. Jn 15:1–8), *the Paschal*

Mystery is by now grafted onto the history of humanity, onto the history of every individual.

Christian soteriology is a *soteriology of the fullness of life.* Not only is it a soteriology of the *truth* disclosed in Revelation, but at the same time it is also a soteriology of *love.* In a certain sense it is *a soteriology of Divine Love.*

Love, above all, possesses a saving power. The saving power of love, according to the words of Saint Paul in the First Letter to the Corinthians, is greater than that of mere knowledge of the truth: "So faith, hope, love remain, these three; but the greatest of these is love" (1 Cor 13:13). Salvation through love is, at the same time, a sharing in the fullness of truth, and also in the fullness of beauty. All this is in God. All these "treasures of life and of holiness" (*Litanies of the Sacred Heart of Jesus*) God has laid open to man in Jesus Christ.

The fact that Christianity is a religion of salvation is expressed in the *sacramental life of the Church.* Christ, who came "so that they might have life and have it more abundantly" (cf. Jn 10:10), discloses for us the sources of this life. He does so in a particular way through the Paschal Mystery of His Death and Resurrection. Linked to this Mystery are Baptism and the Eucharist, sacraments which create in man the seed of eternal life. In the Paschal Mystery, Christ established the regenerative power of the Sacrament of Reconciliation. After the Resurrection He said to the apostles: "Receive the Holy

Spirit. Whose sins you forgive are forgiven them" (Jn 20:22–23).

The fact that Christianity is a religion of salvation is also expressed in *worship*. At the center of the *opus laudis* (a work or labor of praise) there is the celebration of the Resurrection and of life.

The liturgy of the *Eastern Church* is fundamentally centered on the Resurrection. The *Western Church,* while maintaining the primacy of the Resurrection, has gone further *in the direction of the Passion*. The veneration of Christ's Cross has shaped the history of Christian piety and has inspired the greatest saints emerging over the centuries from the heart of the Church. All of them, beginning with Saint Paul, have been "lovers of the Cross of Christ" (cf. Gal 6:14). A special place among them is occupied by Saint Francis of Assisi, but by many others as well. There is no Christian holiness without devotion to the Passion, just as there is no holiness without the centrality of the Paschal Mystery.

The *Eastern Church* attributes great importance to the *Feast of the Transfiguration*. The saints of the Orthodox Church give outstanding expression to this mystery. The saints of the Catholic Church often received the stigmata, beginning with Saint Francis of Assisi. They bore on their own bodies the sign of their similarity to Christ in His Passion. Thus, over the span of two thousand years, there has come about this *great synthesis of life and of holiness, of which Christ is always the center.*

For all its orientation toward eternal life, toward that happiness which is found in God Himself, Christianity, and especially Western Christianity, never became a religion indifferent to the world. It has always been *open to the world, to its questions, to its anxieties, to its hopes.* This has found particular expression in the Pastoral Constitution on the Church in the Modern World, *Gaudium et Spes,* which sprang from the personal initiative of John XXIII. Before his death, he had enough time to pass it on to the Council, as his personal wish.

Aggiornamento (updating) does not only refer to the renewal of the Church; nor only to the unification of Christians, "that the world may believe" (Jn 17:21). It is also, and above all, God's saving activity on behalf of the world; saving activity centered on this world, a world which is passing away, but which is constantly oriented toward eternity, toward the fullness of life. The Church does not lose sight of this ultimate fullness, toward which Christ leads us. The soteriological nature of the Church is thus confirmed in all aspects of human, temporal life. The Church is the Body of Christ, a living body which gives life to everything.

WHY SO MANY RELIGIONS?

B UT IF GOD WHO IS IN HEAVEN—AND WHO saved and continues to save the world—is One and only One and is He who has revealed Himself in Jesus Christ, why has He allowed so many religions to exist?

Why did He make the search for the truth so arduous, in the midst of a forest of rituals, of beliefs, of revelations, of faiths which have always thrived—and still do today—throughout the world?

———

Y OU SPEAK OF MANY RELIGIONS. INSTEAD I will attempt to show the *common fundamental element* and the *common root* of these religions.

The Council defined the relationship of the Church to non-Christian religions in a specific document that begins with the words *"Nostra aetate"* (*"In our time"*). It is a concise and yet very rich document that authentically hands on the Tradition, faithful to the thought of the earliest Fathers of the Church.

From the beginning, Christian Revelation has viewed the spiritual history of man as including, in some way, all religions, thereby demonstrating *the unity of humankind with regard to the eternal and ultimate destiny of man.* The Council document speaks of this unity and links it with the current trend to bring humanity closer together through the resources available to our civilization. The Church sees the promotion of this unity as one of its duties: *"There is only one community and it consists of all peoples.* They have only one origin, since God inhabited the entire earth with the whole human race. And they have one ultimate destiny, God, whose providence, goodness, and plan for salvation extend to all. . . . Men *turn to various religions to solve mysteries of the human condition,* which today, as in earlier times, burden people's hearts: the nature of man; the meaning and purpose of life; good and evil; the origin and purpose of suffering; the way to true happiness; death; judgment and retribution after death; and finally, the ultimate ineffable mystery which is the origin and destiny of our existence. From ancient times up to today all the various peoples have shared and continue to share an awareness of that enigmatic power that is present throughout the course of things and throughout the events of human life, and, in which, at times, even the Supreme Divinity or the Father is recognizable. This awareness and recognition imbue life with an intimate religious sense. Religions that are tied up with cultural progress strive to solve these issues with more refined concepts and a more precise language" (*Nostra Aetate* 1–2).

Here the Council document brings us to the *Far East*—first of all to Asia, a continent where the Church's missionary activity, carried out since the times of the apostles, has borne, we must recognize, very modest fruit. It is well known that only a small percentage of the population on what is the largest continent believes in Christ.

This does not mean that the Church's missionary effort has lapsed—quite the opposite: that effort has been and still remains intense. And yet *the tradition of very ancient cultures*, antedating Christianity, *remains very strong in the East*. Even if faith in Christ reaches hearts and minds, the negative connotations associated with the image of life in Western society (the so-called Christian society) present a considerable obstacle to the acceptance of the Gospel. Mahatma Gandhi, Indian and Hindu, pointed this out many times, in his deeply evangelical manner. He was disillusioned with the ways in which Christianity was expressed in the political and social life of nations. Could a man who fought for the liberation of his great nation from colonial dependence accept Christianity in the same form as it had been imposed on his country by those same colonial powers?

The Second Vatican Council realized this difficulty. This is why the document on the relations between the Church and *Hinduism* and other religions of the Far

East is so important. We read: "In *Hinduism* men explore the divine mystery and express it through an endless bounty of myths and through penetrating philosophical insight. They seek freedom from the anguish of our human condition, either by way of the ascetic life, profound meditation, or by taking refuge in God with love and trust. The various schools of *Buddhism* recognize the radical inadequacy of this malleable world and teach a way by which men, with devout and trusting hearts, can become capable either of reaching a state of perfect liberation, or of attaining, by their own efforts or through higher help, supreme illumination" (*Nostra Aetate* 2).

Further along, the Council remarks that *"The Catholic Church rejects nothing that is true and holy in these religions. The Church has a high regard for their conduct and way of life, for those precepts and doctrines which, although differing on many points from that which the Church believes and propounds, often reflect a ray of that truth which enlightens all men.* However, the Church proclaims, and is bound to proclaim that *Christ is 'the way and the truth and the life'* [Jn 14:6], in whom men must find the fullness of religious life and in whom God has reconciled everything to Himself" (*Nostra Aetate* 2).

The words of the Council recall the conviction, long rooted in the Tradition, of the existence of the so-called *semina Verbi* (seeds of the Word), present in all religions. In the light of this conviction, the Church seeks to identify the *semina Verbi* present in the great traditions of the

Far East, in order to trace a common path against the backdrop of the needs of the contemporary world. We can affirm that here the position of the Council is inspired by a *truly universal concern.* The Church is guided by the faith that *God the Creator wants to save all humankind in Jesus Christ,* the only mediator between God and humankind, inasmuch as He is the Redeemer of all humankind. The Paschal Mystery is equally available to all, and, through it, the way to eternal salvation is also open to all.

In another passage the Council says that the Holy Spirit works effectively even outside the visible structure of the Church (cf. *Lumen Gentium* 13), making use of these very *semina Verbi,* that constitute a kind of *common soteriological root present in all religions.*

I have been convinced of this on numerous occasions, both while *visiting the countries of the Far East* and while meeting representatives of those religions, especially during the historic *meeting at Assisi,* where we found ourselves gathered together praying for peace.

Thus, instead of marveling at the fact that Providence allows such a great variety of religions, we should be amazed at the number of common elements found within them.

At this point it would be helpful to recall all the *primitive religions,* the *animistic religions* which stress ancestor worship. It seems that those who practice them are particularly close to Christianity, and among them, the Church's missionaries also find it easier to speak a common language. Is there, perhaps, in this veneration of ancestors a kind of preparation for the Christian faith in the Communion of Saints, in which all believers—whether living or dead—form a single community, a single body? And faith in the Communion of Saints is, ultimately, faith in Christ, who alone is the source of life and of holiness for all. There is nothing strange, then, that the African and Asian animists would become believers in Christ more easily than followers of the great *religions of the Far East.*

As the Council also noted, these last religions possess the *characteristics of a system.* They are *systems of worship* and also *ethical systems,* with a strong emphasis on good and evil. Certainly among these belong Chinese Confucianism and Taoism: Tao means eternal truth—something similar to the "Word"—which is reflected in the action of man by means of truth and moral good. The religions of the Far East have contributed greatly to the history of morality and culture, forming a national identity in the Chinese, Indians, Japanese, and Tibetans, and also in the peoples of Southeast Asia and the archipelagoes of the Pacific Ocean.

Some of these peoples come from age-old cultures. The indigenous peoples of Australia boast a history tens of thousands of years old, and their ethnic and religious tradition is older than that of Abraham and Moses.

Christ came into the world for all these peoples. He redeemed them all and has His own ways of reaching each of them in the present eschatological phase of salvation history. In fact, in those regions, many accept Him and many more have an implicit faith in Him (cf. Heb 11:6).

BUDDHA?

BEFORE MOVING ON TO MONOTHEISM, TO THE two other religions (Judaism and Islam) which worship one God, I would like to ask you to speak more fully on the subject of Buddhism. Essentially—as you well know—it offers a "doctrine of salvation" that seems increasingly to fascinate many Westerners as an "alternative" to Christianity or as a sort of "complement" to it, at least in terms of certain ascetic and mystical techniques.

YES, YOU ARE RIGHT AND I AM GRATEFUL TO you for this question. Among the religions mentioned in the Council document *Nostra Aetate,* it is necessary to pay special attention to *Buddhism,* which from a certain point of view, like Christianity, is a religion of salvation. Nevertheless, it needs to be said right away that the doctrines of salvation in Buddhism and Christianity are opposed.

. . .

The *Dalai Lama,* spiritual leader of the Tibetans, is a well-known figure in the West. I have met him a few times. He brings Buddhism to people of the Christian West, stirring up interest both in Buddhist spirituality and in its methods of praying. I also had the chance to meet the Buddhist "patriarch" in Bangkok, Thailand, and among the monks that surrounded him there were several, for example, who came from the United States. Today we are seeing a certain *diffusion of Buddhism in the West.*

The *Buddhist doctrine of salvation* constitutes the central point, or rather the only point, of this system. Nevertheless, both the Buddhist tradition and the methods deriving from it have an almost exclusively *negative soteriology.*

The "enlightenment" experienced by Buddha comes down to the conviction that the world is bad, that it is the source of evil and of suffering for man. To liberate oneself from this evil, one must free oneself from this world, necessitating a break with the ties that join us to external reality—ties existing in our human nature, in our psyche, in our bodies. The more we are liberated from these ties, the more we become indifferent to what is in the world, and the more we are freed from suffering, from the evil that has its source in the world.

Do we draw near to God in this way? This is not mentioned in the "enlightenment" conveyed by Buddha. Buddhism is in large measure an *"atheistic"* system. We do not free ourselves from evil through the good which comes from God; we liberate ourselves only through detachment from the world, which is bad. The fullness of such a detachment is not union with God, but what is called nirvana, a state of perfect indifference with regard to the world. *To save oneself* means, above all, to free oneself from evil by becoming *indifferent to the world, which is the source of evil.* This is the culmination of the spiritual process.

At various times, attempts to link this method with the Christian mystics have been made—whether it is with those from northern Europe (Eckhart, Tauler, Suso, Ruysbroeck) or the later Spanish mystics (Saint Teresa of Avila, Saint John of the Cross). But when Saint John of the Cross, in the *Ascent of Mount Carmel* and in the *Dark Night of the Soul,* speaks of the need for purification, for detachment from the world of the senses, he does not conceive of that detachment as an end in itself. "To arrive at what now you do not enjoy, you must go where you do not enjoy. To reach what you do not know, you must go where you do not know. To come into possession of what you do not have, you must go where now you have nothing" (*Ascent of Mount Carmel,* 1. 13. 11). In Eastern Asia these classic texts of Saint John of the Cross have been, at times, interpreted as a confirmation of Eastern ascetic methods. But this Doctor of the Church does not merely propose detachment from the world. He proposes detachment from the world in order to unite oneself to that which is outside of the world—by this I do not mean nirvana, but a personal God. Union with Him comes about not only through purification, but through love.

Carmelite mysticism begins at the point where the reflections of Buddha end, together with his instructions for the spiritual life. In the active and passive purification of the human soul, in those specific nights of the senses and the spirit, Saint John of the Cross sees, above all, the preparation necessary for the human soul to be permeated with the living flame of love. And this is also the title of his major work—*The Living Flame of Love.*

Therefore, despite similar aspects, there is a fundamental difference. *Christian mysticism* from every period—beginning with the era of the Fathers of the Eastern and Western Church, to the great theologians of Scholasticism (such as Saint Thomas Aquinas), to the northern European mystics, to the Carmelite mystics—is not born of a purely negative "enlightenment." It is not born of an awareness of the evil which exists in man's attachment to the world through the senses, the intellect, and the spirit. Instead, Christian mysticism is born of the *Revelation of the living God.* This God opens Himself to union with man, arousing in him the capacity to be united with Him, especially by means of the theological virtues—faith, hope, and, above all, love.

Christian mysticism in every age up to our own—including the mysticism of marvelous men of action

like Vincent de Paul, John Bosco, Maximilian Kolbe—
has built up and continues to build up Christianity
in its most essential element. It also builds up the
Church as a community of faith, hope, and charity. It
builds up civilization, particularly "Western civilization," which is marked by a *positive approach to the world,*
and which developed thanks to the achievements of
science and technology, two branches of knowledge
rooted both in the ancient Greek philosophical tradition
and in Judeo-Christian Revelation. The truth about
God the Creator of the world and about Christ the
Redeemer is a powerful force which inspires a positive
attitude toward creation and provides a constant impe-
tus to strive for its transformation and perfection.

The Second Vatican Council has amply confirmed
this truth. To indulge in a negative attitude toward the
world, in the conviction that it is only a source of suffering for man and that he therefore must break away from
it, is negative not only because it is unilateral but also
because it is fundamentally contrary to the development
of both man himself and the world, which the Creator
has given and entrusted to man as his task.

We read in *Gaudium et Spes:* "Therefore, the *world*
which [the Council] has in mind is the world *of men, of
the entire human family* considered in the context of all
realities; the world which is the theater of human history and which bears the marks of humanity's struggles, its defeats, and its victories; the world which the
Christians believe has been created and is sustained by
the Creator's love, a world enslaved by sin but liberated

by the crucified and resurrected Christ in order to defeat evil, and destined, *according to the divine plan, to be transformed and to reach its fulfillment*" (*Gaudium et Spes* 2).

These words indicate how between Christianity and the religions of the Far East, in particular Buddhism, there is an essentially different way of perceiving the world. For Christians, the world is God's creation, redeemed by Christ. It is in the world that man meets God. Therefore he does not need to attain such an absolute detachment in order to find himself in the mystery of his deepest self. For Christianity, it does not make sense to speak of the world as a "radical" evil, since at the beginning of the world we find God the Creator who loves His creation, a God who "gave his only Son, so that everyone who believes in him might not perish but might have eternal life" (Jn 3:16).

For this reason it is not inappropriate *to caution* those Christians who enthusiastically *welcome certain ideas originating in the religious traditions of the Far East*—for example, techniques and methods of meditation and ascetical practice. In some quarters these have become fashionable, and are accepted rather uncritically. First one should know one's own spiritual heritage well and consider whether it is right to set it aside lightly. Here we need to recall, if only in passing, the brief but important document of the Congregation for the Doctrine of the Faith "on certain aspects of Christian meditation" (10/15/1989). Here we find a clear answer to the question "whether and how [Christian prayer] can be enriched by methods of meditation originating in different religions and cultures" (n. 3).

A separate issue is the *return of ancient gnostic ideas under the guise of the so-called New Age.* We cannot delude ourselves that this will lead toward a renewal of religion. It is only a new way of practicing gnosticism— that attitude of the spirit that, in the name of a profound knowledge of God, results in distorting His Word and replacing it with purely human words. Gnosticism never completely abandoned the realm of Christianity. Instead, it has always existed side by side with Christianity, sometimes taking the shape of a philosophical movement, but more often assuming the characteristics of a religion or para-religion in distinct, if not declared, conflict with all that is essentially Christian.

Muhammad?

A VERY DIFFERENT DISCUSSION, OBVIOUSLY, is the one that leads us to the synagogues and mosques, where those who worship the One God assemble.

Y ES, CERTAINLY IT IS A DIFFERENT CASE when we come to these *great monotheistic* religions, beginning with *Islam*. In the Declaration *Nostra Aetate* we read: "The Church also has a high regard for the Muslims, who worship one God, living and subsistent, merciful and omnipotent, the Creator of heaven and earth" (*Nostra Aetate* 3). As a result of their monotheism, believers in Allah are particularly close to us.

I remember an event from my youth. In the convent of the Church of Saint Mark in Florence, we were look-ing at the frescoes by Fra Angelico. At a certain point a man joined us who, after sharing his admiration for the work of this great religious artist, immediately added: "But nothing can compare to our magnificent Muslim monotheism." His statement did not prevent us from continuing the visit and the conversation in a friendly tone. It was on that occasion that I got a kind of first taste of the dialogue between Christianity and Islam, which we have tried to develop systematically in the post-conciliar period.

Whoever knows the Old and New Testaments, and then reads the Koran, clearly sees the *process by which it completely reduces Divine Revelation*. It is impossible not to note the movement away from what God said about Himself, first in the Old Testament through the Prophets, and then finally in the New Testament through His Son. In Islam all the richness of God's self-revelation, which constitutes the heritage of the Old and New Testaments, has definitely been set aside.

Some of the most beautiful names in the human language are given to the God of the Koran, but He is ultimately a God outside of the world, a God who is *only Majesty, never Emmanuel*, God-with-us. *Islam is not a religion of redemption.* There is no room for the Cross and the Resurrection. Jesus is mentioned, but only as a prophet who prepares for the last prophet, Muhammad. There is also mention of Mary, His Virgin Mother, but the tragedy of redemption is completely absent. For this reason not only the theology but also the anthropology of Islam is very distant from Christianity.

. . .

Nevertheless, *the religiosity of Muslims deserves respect.* It is impossible not to admire, for example, their *fidelity to prayer.* The image of believers in Allah who, without caring about time or place, fall to their knees and immerse themselves in prayer remains a model for all *those who invoke* the true God, in particular for those Christians who, having deserted their magnificent cathedrals, pray only a little or not at all.

The Council has also called for the Church to have a *dialogue* with followers of the "Prophet," and the Church has proceeded to do so. We read in *Nostra Aetate:* "Even if over the course of centuries Christians and Muslims have had more than a few dissensions and quarrels, this sacred Council now urges all to forget the past and to work toward mutual understanding as well as toward the preservation and promotion of social justice, moral welfare, peace, and freedom for the benefit of all mankind" (*Nostra Aetate* 3).

From this point of view, as I have already mentioned, the meetings for prayer held at Assisi (especially that for peace in Bosnia, in 1993), certainly played a significant role. Also worthwhile were my meetings with the followers of Islam during my numerous apostolic trips to Africa and Asia, where sometimes, in a given country, the majority of the citizens were Muslims. Despite this, the Pope was welcomed with great hospitality and was listened to with similar graciousness.

The trip I made to Morocco at the invitation of King Hassan II can certainly be defined as a historic event. It was not simply a courtesy visit, but an event of a truly pastoral nature. The encounter with the young people at Casablanca Stadium (1985) was unforgettable. The openness of the young people to the Pope's words was striking when he spoke of faith in the one God. It was certainly an unprecedented event.

Nevertheless, concrete difficulties are not lacking. In countries where *fundamentalist movements* come to power, human rights and the principle of religious freedom are unfortunately interpreted in a very one-sided way—religious freedom comes to mean freedom to impose on all citizens the "true religion." In these countries the situation of Christians is sometimes terribly disturbing. Fundamentalist attitudes of this nature make reciprocal contacts very difficult. All the same, the Church remains always open to dialogue and cooperation.

JUDAISM?

A T THIS POINT IT IS NATURAL TO ASSUME THAT
Your Holiness intends to speak of Judaism.

———————

T HAT IS RIGHT. THROUGH THE AMAZING
plurality of religions, arranged as it were in con-
centric circles, we come to the religion that is closest
to our own—that of the people of God of the Old Testament.

The words from the Declaration *Nostra Aetate* represent a turning point. The Council says: "The Church
of Christ, in fact, recognizes that according to the
divine mystery of salvation the origins of the Church's
faith and election are already found in the Patriarchs,
Moses, and the Prophets. . . . The Church, then, can
forget neither that it received the revelation of the Old
Testament through that people with whom God, in
his ineffable mercy, made the Ancient Covenant, nor

can the Church forget that it draws sustenance from the root of that good olive tree onto which have been grafted the wild shoots, the Gentiles. . . . Therefore, since the spiritual patrimony common to Christians and Jews is so great, this Sacred Council recommends and promotes a mutual understanding and respect, which can be obtained above all through biblical study and fraternal discussion" (*Nostra Aetate* 4).

The words of the Council's Declaration reflect the experience of many people, both Jews and Christians. They reflect *my personal experience* as well, from the very first years of my life in my hometown. I remember, above all, the Wadowice elementary school, where at least a fourth of the pupils in my class were Jewish. I should mention my friendship at school with one of them, Jerzy Kluger—a friendship that has lasted from my school days to the present. I can vividly remember the Jews who gathered every Saturday at the synagogue behind our school. Both religious groups, Catholics and Jews, were united, I presume, by the awareness that they prayed to the same God. Despite their different languages, prayers in the church and in the synagogue were based to a considerable degree on the same texts.

Then came the Second World War, with its concentration camps and systematic extermination. First and foremost, the sons and daughters of the Jewish nation were condemned for no other reason than that they were Jewish. Even if only indirectly, whoever lived in Poland at that time came into contact with this reality.

Therefore, this was also a personal experience of mine, an experience I carry with me even today. Auschwitz, perhaps the most meaningful symbol of the *Holocaust of the Jewish people,* shows to what lengths a system constructed on principles of racial hatred and greed for power can go. To this day, Auschwitz does not cease to admonish, reminding us that *anti-Semitism is a great sin against humanity,* that all racial hatred inevitably leads to the trampling of human dignity.

I would like to return to the synagogue at Wadowice. It was destroyed by the Germans and no longer exists today. A few years ago Jerzy came to me to say that the place where the synagogue had stood should be honored with a special commemorative plaque. I must admit that in that moment we both felt a deep emotion. We saw faces of people we knew and cared for, and we recalled those Saturdays of our childhood and adolescence when the Jewish community of Wadowice gathered for prayer. I promised him I would gladly send a personal note as a sign of my solidarity and spiritual union on the occasion of such an important event. And so I did. It was Jerzy himself who brought that letter to my fellow citizens in Wadowice. That trip was not easy for him. All the members of his family who had remained in that small town had died at Auschwitz. His visit to Wadowice for the unveiling of the plaque in commemoration of the local synagogue was his first in fifty years. . . .

The words of *Nostra Aetate,* as I have said, reflect the experience of many. I think back to *the time of my pastoral work in Kraków.* Kraków, and especially the Kazimierz neighborhood, retain many traces of Jewish culture and tradition. In Kazimierz, before the war, there were several dozen synagogues which were in some sense great cultural monuments as well. As Archbishop of Kraków, I was in close contact with the city's Jewish community. I enjoyed very cordial relations with the head of that community, which continued even after I came to Rome.

After my election to the See of Saint Peter, I have continued to cherish these deeply significant ties. On my pastoral journeys around the world I always try to meet representatives of the Jewish community. But a truly exceptional experience for me was certainly my *visit to the synagogue of Rome.* The history of the Jews in Rome is a unique chapter in the history of the Jewish people, a chapter closely linked for that matter to The Acts of the Apostles. During that memorable visit, I spoke of the Jews as our *elder brothers in the faith.* These words were an expression both of the Council's teaching, and a profound conviction on the part of the Church. The Second Vatican Council did not dwell on this subject at length, but what it did affirm embraces an immense reality which is not only religious but also cultural.

This extraordinary people continues to bear signs of its divine election. I said this to an Israeli politician once and he readily agreed, but was quick to add: *"If only it could cost less! . . ."* Israel has truly paid a high price for its "election." Perhaps because of this, Israel has become more similar to the Son of man, who, according to the flesh, was also a son of Israel. The two thousandth anniversary of His coming to the world will be a celebration for Jews as well.

I am pleased that my ministry in the See of Saint Peter has taken place during the period following the Second Vatican Council, when the insights which inspired the Declaration *Nostra Aetate* are finding concrete expression in various ways. Thus the way two great moments of divine election—the Old and the New Covenants—are drawing closer together.

The New Covenant has its roots in the Old. The time when the people of the Old Covenant will be able to see themselves as part of the New is, naturally, a question to be left to the Holy Spirit. We, as human beings, try only not to put obstacles in the way. The form this "not putting obstacles" takes is certainly dialogue between Christians and Jews, which, on the Church's part, is being carried forward by the Pontifical Council for Promoting Christian Unity.

. . .

I am also pleased that as a result of the peace process currently taking place, despite setbacks and obstacles, in the Middle East, and thanks also to the initiative of the State of Israel, it became possible to *establish diplomatic relations between the Apostolic See and Israel*. As for the recognition of the State of Israel, it is important to reaffirm that I myself never had any doubts in this regard.

Once, after the conclusion of one of my meetings with the Jewish community, someone present said: "I want to thank the Pope for all that the Catholic Church has done over the last two thousand years to make the true God known."

These words indirectly indicate how the New Covenant serves to fulfill all that is rooted in the vocation of Abraham, in God's covenant with Israel at Sinai, and in the whole rich heritage of the inspired Prophets who, hundreds of years before that fulfillment, pointed in the Sacred Scriptures to the One whom God would send in the "fullness of time" (cf. Gal 4:4).

A Minority by the
Year 2000

P ARDON ME, YOUR HOLINESS, BUT MY ROLE
(which gives me great honor but also a certain
responsibility) is also that of a respectful "provocateur"
with regard to questions—even troubling ones—which
are also present among Catholics.

I will continue, then, by observing how you have
frequently recalled—with an awareness of the symbolic importance of the event—the approach of the
third millennium of the Redemption. According to
statistical projections, by the year 2000, for the first
time in history, Muslims will outnumber Catholics.
Already Hindus alone are more numerous than Protestants and Orthodox Greeks and Slavs combined. In
your pastoral journeys around the world, you have
often visited places where believers in Christ, and
Catholics in particular, are a small and even shrinking
minority.

How do you feel when faced with this reality, after twenty centuries of evangelization? What divine plan do you see at work here?

I THINK THAT SUCH A VIEW OF THE PROBLEM arises from a somewhat simplistic interpretation of the matter. In reality, the essence goes far deeper, as I have already tried to explain in my response to the preceding question. Here statistics are not useful—we are speaking of *values which are not quantifiable.*

To tell the truth, the sociology of religion—although useful in other areas—does not help much here. As a basis for assessment, the criteria for measurement which it provides do not help when considering people's interior attitude. *No statistic* aiming at a quantitative measurement of faith (for example, the number of people who participate in religious ceremonies) will get to the heart of the matter. *Here numbers alone are not enough.*

The question you ask—albeit "provocatively," as you say—amounts to this: let us count the number of Muslims in the world, or the number of Hindus, *let us count the number of Catholics,* or Christians in general, and we can determine which religion is in the majority, *which has a future ahead of it,* and which instead seems to belong only to the past, or is undergoing a systematic process of decomposition and decline.

From the point of view of the Gospel the issue is completely different. Christ says: *"Do not be afraid any longer, little flock,* for your Father is pleased to give you the kingdom" (Lk 12:32). I think that in these words Christ best responds to this problem that some find troubling and that is raised in your question. Jesus goes even further when He asks: "When the Son of Man comes, will he find faith on earth?" (cf. Lk 18:8).

Both this question and the earlier saying about the little flock indicate the profound realism which inspired Jesus in dealing with His apostles. *He did not prepare them for easy success.* He spoke clearly, He spoke of the persecutions that awaited those who would believe in Him. At the same time, *He established a solid foundation for the faith.* "The Father was pleased to give the Kingdom" to those twelve men from Galilee, and through them to all humanity. He forewarned them that the mission He sent them on would involve opposition and persecution because He Himself had been persecuted: "If they persecuted me, they will also persecute you." But He hastened to add: "If they kept my word, they will also keep yours" (cf. Jn 15:20).

Since my youth I have felt that the heart of the Gospel is contained in these words. *The Gospel is not a promise of easy success.* It does not promise a comfortable life to anyone. It makes demands and, at the same time, it is *a great promise*—the promise of eternal life for man, who is subject to the law of death, and the promise of victory through faith for man, who is subject to many trials and setbacks.

The Gospel contains a *fundamental paradox:* to find life, one must lose life; to be born, one must die; to save oneself, one must take up the cross. This is the essential truth of the Gospel, which always and everywhere is bound to meet with man's protest.

Always and everywhere the Gospel will be a challenge to human weakness. But precisely in this challenge lies all its power. Man, perhaps, subconsciously waits for such a challenge; *indeed, man feels the inner need to transcend himself.* Only in transcending himself does man become fully human (cf. Blaise Pascal, *Pensées,* ed. Brunschvicg, 434: "Apprenez que l'homme passe infiniment l'homme").

This is the most profound truth about man. *Christ is the first to know this truth.* He truly knows "that which is in every man" (cf. Jn 2:25). With His Gospel He has touched the intimate truth of man. He has touched it first of all with His Cross. Pilate, who, pointing to the Nazarene crowned with thorns after His scourging, said, "Behold, the man!" (Jn 19:5), did not realize that he was proclaiming an essential truth, expressing that which always and everywhere remains the heart of evangelization.

WHAT IS THE "NEW EVANGELIZATION"?

I WOULD LIKE TO ASK YOU TO DWELL A MOMENT on that last expression, which continually recurs in your teaching, in your exhortations—"evangelization" (or, rather, "new evangelization"). For the present Pope this seems to be the primary duty of Christians at the end of the twentieth century.

T HE CALL FOR A GREAT RELAUNCHING OF *evangelization* enters again and again into the present life of the Church in a number of ways. In truth, it has never been absent. "Woe to me if I do not preach the Gospel!" (cf. 1 Cor 9:16). This statement of Paul of Tarsus has been true for every age in the history of the Church. Paul, a converted Pharisee, was untiringly driven by that "woe." The Mediterranean world in which he lived heard his message—the Good News of salvation in Jesus Christ. And that world began to reflect on the significance of such a message. Many people followed the apostle. We must never forget the mysterious call that drove Saint Paul to cross the border between Asia Minor and Europe (cf. Acts 16:9–10). This led to the *first evangelization of Europe.*

The Gospel's encounter with the Greek world proved to be exceptionally fruitful. Among those whom Paul succeeded in gathering around him, those who heard him at the Areopagus in Athens merit special attention. An analysis of *Saint Paul's speech at the Areopagus* reveals that it is a masterpiece of its kind. What the apostle said and how he said it illustrate his genius as a preacher of the Gospel. We know that the day ended in failure. As long as Paul spoke of an unknown God, his listeners followed him because they detected in his words something that spoke to their own religious sensibilities. But when he mentioned the Resurrection, they immediately rose up in protest. The apostle then understood that the mystery of salvation in Christ would not be easily accepted by the Greeks, accustomed as they were to mythology and to various forms of philosophical speculation. Nevertheless, he did not lay down his weapons. After his setback at Athens, he nonetheless continued with *holy stubbornness* to proclaim the Gospel to every creature. This holy stubbornness finally led him to Rome, where he met his death.

Thus, the Gospel was carried beyond the narrow confines of Jerusalem and Palestine, beginning its march to the *confines of the then-known world.* The words Paul preached in person he reiterated in his Letters. These Letters attest to the fact that the apostle left behind him, wherever he went, living communities in which he did not cease to be present as a witness to the Crucified and Risen Christ.

The evangelization undertaken by the apostles laid the foundations for the building of the spiritual structure of the Church, becoming the *seed* and, in a certain sense, the *model* valid for every age. Following the apostles' footsteps, the second- and third-generation disciples continued the work of evangelization. This was an *heroic age,* the age of Saint Ignatius of Antioch, Saint Polycarp, and many other outstanding martyrs.

Evangelization is not only the Church's living teaching, the first proclamation of the faith (*kērygma*) and instruction, formation in the faith (catechesis); it is also the entire *wide-ranging commitment to reflect on revealed truth,* a commitment which has been expressed from the very beginning in the *works of the Fathers* in the East and in the West. And when this teaching had to confront the speculations of Gnosticism or various emerging heresies, it could be polemical.

Evangelization was, in particular, the driving force of the various councils. In the early centuries, if the Church's encounter with the Greek world had not taken place, the Council of Jerusalem, held by the apostles themselves around the year 50 (cf. Acts 15), would probably have been enough. The ecumenical councils that followed sprang from the need to express the truth of the revealed faith in *meaningful and convincing language* to people living in a Greek world.

All of this belongs to the *history of evangelization,* a history that developed in the *encounter of the Gospel with the culture of each epoch.* It must be recognized that besides providing the basis for theological and philosophical doctrines of the first millennium, the Fathers of the Church played a fundamental role in the evangelization of the world. Christ had said: "Go into the whole world" (Mk 16:15). As the known world slowly expanded, the Church also faced ever new challenges in evangelization.

The first millennium saw the Church's encounter with the many peoples who, in the course of their migration, came into contact with centers of Christianity. There they accepted the faith and became Christians, even if very often they were not able to comprehend the mystery in its fullness. Thus many of them fell into Arianism, which denied the equality of the Son with the Father, and they fought for the victory of this heresy in the Christian world. These were not only ideological disputes; there was a constant struggle to preserve the Gospel itself. Yet, throughout these controversies, the words of Christ continued to echo: "Go, therefore, and make disciples of all nations" (cf. Mt 28:19). "*Ad gentes!*" These words, uttered by the Redeemer of the world, have borne astonishing *fruit.*

. . .

One of the greatest events in the history of evangelization was certainly the mission of the two brothers from Thessalonica, Saint Cyril and Saint Methodius. They were the apostles of the Slavs—they introduced the Gospel and at the same time laid the foundations of Slavic culture. In some measure, the Slavic peoples are indebted to these saints for their liturgical and literary language. Both were active during the ninth century between Constantinople and Rome, working on behalf of the unity of the Eastern and Western Church, even though this unity had already begun to crumble. In the vast regions of central and southern Europe the heritage of their evangelization lives on. To this day, many Slavic nations acknowledge them not only as teachers of the faith but also as fathers of their culture.

A great new wave of evangelization began at the end of the fifteenth century, originating above all in Spain and Portugal. This is all the more extraordinary because it was precisely in that period, after the schism between the Eastern and Western Churches in the eleventh century, that the tragic division in the West was taking place. By now the great splendor of the medieval papacy was past; the Protestant Reformation was spreading rapidly. At the very moment in which the Roman Church was losing the peoples north of the Alps, Providence opened up new prospects. With the *discovery of America,* the evangelization of that entire hemisphere, from north to south, was set in motion. We recently celebrated the five hundredth anniversary of this evangelization, with the intention not only of commemorating an event of the past but of considering our present obligations in light of the work carried out by the heroic missionaries, especially religious, who labored throughout the Americas.

The missionary zeal, which was so apparent on the other side of the Atlantic with the discovery of a new continent, also elicited ecclesial initiatives aimed at the East. The sixteenth century is also the century of Saint Francis Xavier, whose missionary achievement was directed to the East—India and Japan, in particular. He was enormously effective there, despite the strong resistance he encountered from cultures which those great peoples had developed over thousands of years. It was necessary to set about the work of *inculturation,* as Father Matteo Ricci, the apostle of China, proposed, if Christianity was to penetrate the soul of these peoples. I have already mentioned that only a small percentage of Asia is Christian; nonetheless this "little flock" is certainly part of the Kingdom given by the Father to the apostles through Christ. The *vitality of some of the Asian Churches* is remarkable—once again this is the result of persecution. It is particularly true in Korea, Vietnam, and, recently, in China as well.

The awareness that the entire Church is *in statu missionis* (in a state of mission) was strongly felt in the last century, as it is today, especially among the ancient

Churches of western Europe. In the past (for example, in France), fully half of the priests in some dioceses went off to the missions.

The encyclical *Redemptoris Missio,* published a few years ago, embraces this distant and recent past, beginning with the Areopagus in Athens and continuing up to our own time, in which episodes similar to the one at the Areopagus have occurred over and over again. The Church evangelizes, the Church proclaims Christ, who is the Way, the Truth, and the Life; Christ who is the one mediator between God and man. And despite its human weakness, the Church never tires of proclaiming Christ. The great missionary wave that arose in the last century was directed toward all continents and, in particular, toward *Africa.* Today on that continent we meet a fully established indigenous Church. There are many black bishops. Africa is becoming a continent of missionary vocations. And vocations—by the grace of God—are not lacking. As they are diminishing in Europe, the more they are growing in Africa and Asia.

Perhaps, one day, the words of Cardinal Hyacinth Thiandoum, who foresaw the possibility that the Old World would be evangelized by black missionaries, will prove true. Again, we must ask ourselves if this is not evidence of *the Church's ever renewed vitality.* I bring this up in order to throw a different light on the somewhat troubling question of the number of Christians, and of Catholics in particular. Truly, *there are no grounds for losing hope.* If the world is not Catholic from a denominational point of view, it is nonetheless profoundly permeated by the Gospel. We can even say that the mystery of the Church, the Body of Christ, is in some way invisibly present in it.

Against the spirit of the world, the Church takes up anew each day a struggle that is none other than *the struggle for the world's soul.* If in fact, on the one hand, the Gospel and evangelization are present in this world, on the other, there is also present *a powerful antievangelization* which is well organized and has the means to vigorously oppose the Gospel and evangelization. The struggle for the soul of the contemporary world is at its height where the spirit of this world seems strongest. In this sense the encyclical *Redemptoris Missio* speaks of *modern Areopagi.* Today these *Areopagi* are the worlds of science, culture, and media; these are the worlds of writers and artists, the worlds where the intellectual elite are formed.

In its ever renewed encounter with man, evangelization is *linked to generational change.* Generations come and go which have distanced themselves from Christ and the Church, which have accepted a secular model of thinking and living or upon which such a model has been imposed. Meanwhile, the Church is always looking toward the future. She constantly *goes out to meet new generations.* And new generations clearly seem to be accepting with enthusiasm what their elders seemed to have rejected.

What does this mean? It means that *Christ is forever young.* It means that the Holy Spirit is incessantly at work. Christ's words are striking: "My Father is at work until now, so I am at work" (Jn 5:17). The Father and the Son are at work in the Holy Spirit, who is the Spirit of truth, and truth does not cease to fascinate man, especially the hearts of the young. Therefore we should not consider statistics alone. For Christ, works of charity are important. Despite all of the losses the Church has suffered, it *does not cease to look toward the future with hope.* Such hope is a sign of the power of the Spirit. *And the power of the Spirit must always be judged in the light of these words of the Apostle: "Woe to me if I do not preach the Gospel!"* (cf. 1 Cor 9:16).

Ten years after the Council, the *Synod of Bishops on the theme of evangelization* was convened. It bore fruit in the apostolic exhortation of Paul VI, *Evangelii Nuntiandi.* It is not an encyclical, but in its great importance it perhaps surpasses many encyclicals. It can be considered the interpretation of the Council's teaching on the essential duty of the Church: "Woe to me if I do not preach the Gospel!"

As the year 2000 approaches, our world feels an urgent need for the Gospel. Perhaps we feel this need precisely because the world seems to be distancing itself from the Gospel, or rather because the world has not yet drawn near to the Gospel. The *first case*—the move away from the Gospel—is particularly true of the "Old World," especially of Europe; the *second* is true of Asia, the Far East, and Africa. The expression *new evangelization* was popularized by *Evangelii Nuntiandi* as a response to the

new challenges that the contemporary world creates for the
mission of the Church.

It is symptomatic that *Redemptoris Missio* speaks of a
new spring of evangelization, and it is even more significant that this encyclical was received with great satisfac-
tion, even enthusiasm, in various quarters. Following
Evangelii Nuntiandi, Redemptoris Missio represents a new
synthesis of the Church's teaching about evangelization
in the contemporary world.

The encyclical sets forth the *main problems;* it identi-
fies by name the *obstacles* which beset the road of evangelization; it clarifies certain *concepts,* which at times are
misused, especially in journalistic language; finally, it
indicates the *areas of the world* (for example, the post-
Communist countries) where the truth of the Gospel is
anxiously awaited. For these countries, which have had
a long history of Christianity, a kind of "re-evangeliza-
tion" is called for.

The new evangelization has nothing in common with
what various publications have insinuated when speaking of *restoration,* or when advancing the accusation of
proselytism, or when unilaterally or tendentiously calling
for *pluralism* and *tolerance.* A careful reading of the
Council's decree *Dignitatis Humanae* on religious freedom can help to clear up these problems, and also to
allay the fears that some are attempting to stir up, perhaps with the aim of depriving the Church of its
courage and enthusiasm in taking up the mission of
evangelization. *The mission of evangelization is an essen-*

tial part of the Church. The Second Vatican Council made this point in a colorful way by affirming that "the Church . . . by her nature is missionary" (*Ad Gentes* 2).

In addition to these objections, which concern evangelization as such and its possibilities in the contemporary world, other objections have been raised concerning the *ways and methods of evangelization.* In 1989 at *Santiago de Compostela,* in Spain, the World Youth Day took place. The response of the young (above all, of young Europeans) was extraordinary. The ancient pilgrimage route leading to the shrine of the apostle Saint James came alive once again. The importance that this shrine and pilgrimages in general have had in Christianity is well known; particularly well known is their role in the formation of European cultural identity. Nevertheless, almost at the very time that this very significant event was taking place, voices were heard saying that *"the dream of Compostela"* belonged irrevocably to the past and that Christian Europe had become a historical phenomenon to be relegated to the history books. That the new evangelization should give rise to such fear in certain quarters of public opinion is something to think about.

In the context of the new evangelization, today's *rediscovery of the authentic values found in popular piety* is very significant. Until fairly recently there was a tendency to look down on popular piety. In our time, however, some of its expressions are experiencing a *true rebirth*—for example, the revival of former pilgrimages and the establishment of new ones. Thus, the unforgettable witness of the gathering at Santiago de Compostela (1989) was followed by the experience of Jasna Góra in Częstochowa (1991). The younger generations in particular are excited about pilgrimages. Not only in the Old World but also in the United States, where, despite the absence of a tradition of pilgrimages to shrines, the World Youth Day in Denver (1993) brought together hundreds of thousands of young believers in Christ.

There exists today *the clear need for a new evangelization. There is the need for a proclamation of the Gospel capable of accompanying man on his pilgrim way, capable of walking alongside the younger generation.* Isn't such a need in itself already a *sign of the approach of the year 2000?* With ever greater frequency pilgrims are looking toward the Holy Land, toward Nazareth, Bethlehem, and Jerusalem. The people of the God of the Old and New Testaments are alive in the younger generation and, at the end of the twentieth century, have the same *experience as Abraham, who followed the voice of God who called him to set out upon the pilgrimage of faith.* And what other phrase in the Gospel do we hear more often than this: "Follow me" (Mt 8:22)? This is a call to the people of today, especially the young, to follow the paths of the Gospel in the direction of a better world.

IS THERE REALLY
HOPE IN THE
YOUNG?

YOUNG PEOPLE HAVE A SPECIAL PLACE IN THE heart of the Holy Father, who often repeats that the whole Church looks to them with particular hope for a new beginning of evangelization.

Your Holiness, is this a realistic hope? Or are we adults only indulging in the illusion that each new generation will be better than ours and all those that came before?

HERE YOU OPEN AN ENORMOUS FIELD FOR discussion and reflection.

What are young people of today like, what are they looking for? It could be said that they are the same as ever. There is something in man which never changes, as the Council recalled in *Gaudium et Spes* (10). This is true especially in the young. But today's youth are also different from those who came before. In the past, the younger generations were shaped by the painful experience of war, of concentration camps, of constant danger. This experience allowed young people—I imagine all over the world, although I have Polish youth in mind—to develop *traits of great heroism.*

I think of the Warsaw uprising in 1944—the desperate revolt of my contemporaries, who sacrificed everything. They laid down their young lives. They wanted to demonstrate that they could live up to their great and demanding heritage. I was a part of that generation and I must say that *the heroism of my contemporaries helped me to define my personal vocation.* Father Konstanty Michalski, one of the great professors at the Jagellonian University in Kraków, wrote the book *Between Heroism and Brutality* after returning from the Sachsenhausen concentration camp. The title of this book captures the climate of the times. Referring to Friar Albert Chmielowski, Michalski recalled the words of the Gospel about the need "to give up one's life" (cf. Jn 15:13). Precisely in that period of absolute contempt for man, when the price of human life had perhaps never been considered so cheap, precisely then each life became precious, acquiring the value of a free gift.

In this regard, *today's young people certainly grow up in a different context.* They do not carry within them the experiences of the Second World War. Furthermore, many of them have not known—or do not remember—the struggle against Communism, against the totalitarian state. They live in freedom, which others have won for them, and have yielded in large part to the consumer culture. This is, in broad terms, the *status of the present situation.*

All the same, it is difficult to say that the young have rejected traditional values, that they have left the Church. The experiences of teachers and pastors *confirm, today no less than yesterday, the idealism present in young people,* even if nowadays it perhaps tends to be expressed mostly in the form of criticism, whereas before it would have translated more simply into duty. In general, the younger generations grow up *in an atmosphere marked by a new positivism,* whereas in Poland, when I was a boy, *romantic traditions* prevailed. The young people with whom I came into contact after I was ordained as a priest believed in these traditions. In the Church and in the Gospel they saw a point of reference which helped them to focus their inner strength, to lead their lives in a way that made sense. I still remember my conversations with those young people who spoke of their relationship with the faith in precisely these terms.

My most memorable experience of that period, when my pastoral activities concentrated above all on the young, was *the discovery of the fundamental importance of youth.* What is youth? It is not only a period of life that corresponds to a certain number of years, it is also *a time given by Providence to every person and given to him as a responsibility.* During that time he searches, like the young man in the Gospel, for answers to basic questions; he searches not only for the meaning of life but also for a concrete way to go about living his life. This is the most fundamental characteristic of youth. Every mentor, beginning with parents, let alone every pastor, must be aware of this characteristic and must know how to identify it in every boy and girl. I will say more: *He must love this fundamental aspect of youth.*

If at every stage of his life man desires to be his own person, to find love, during his youth he desires it even more strongly. The desire to be one's own person, however, must not be understood as a license to do anything, without exception. The young do not want that at all—they are willing to be corrected, they want to be told yes or no. *They need guides,* and they want them close at hand. If they turn to authority figures, they do so because they see in them a wealth of human warmth and a willingness to walk with them along the paths they are following.

Clearly, then, the *fundamental problem of youth is profoundly personal.* In life, youth is when we come to know ourselves. It is also a time of *communion.* Young people, whether boys or girls, know they must live for and with others, they know that their life *has meaning to the extent that it becomes a free gift for others.* Here is the origin of all vocations—whether to priesthood or religious life, or to marriage and family. The call to marriage is also a vocation, a gift from God. *I will never forget a young man, an engineering student in Kraków, who everyone knew aspired with determination to holiness.* This was his life plan. He knew he had been "created for greater things," as Saint Stanislaus Kostka once expressed it. And at the same time, he had no doubt that his vocation was neither to priesthood nor to religious life. He knew he was called to remain in the secular world. Technical work, the study of engineering, was his passion. He sought a companion for his life and sought her on his knees, in prayer. I will never forget the conversation in which, after a special day of retreat, he said to me: "I think that this is the woman who should be my wife, that it is God who has given her to me." It was almost as if he were following not only the voice of his own wishes but above all the voice of God Himself. He knew that all good things come from Him, and he made a good choice. I am speaking of Jerzy Ciesielski, who died in a tragic accident in the Sudan, where he had been invited to teach at the University. The cause for his beatification is already under way.

It is this vocation to love that naturally allows us to draw close to the young. As a priest I realized this very early. I felt almost an inner call in this direction. It is necessary to prepare young people for marriage, it is necessary *to teach them love.* Love is not something that is learned, and yet there is nothing else as important to learn! *As a young priest I learned to love human love.* This has been one of the fundamental themes of my priesthood—my ministry in the pulpit, in the confessional, and also in my writing. If one loves human love, there naturally arises the need to commit oneself completely to the service of "fair love," because love is fair, it is beautiful.

After all, young people are always searching for the beauty in love. They want their love to be beautiful. If they give in to weakness, following models of behavior that can rightly be considered a "scandal in the contemporary world" (and these are, unfortunately, widely diffused models), in the depths of their hearts they still desire a beautiful and pure love. This is as true of boys as it is of girls. Ultimately, they know that only God can give them this love. As a result, they are willing to follow Christ, without caring about the sacrifices this may entail.

As a young priest and pastor I came to this way of looking at young people and at youth, and it has remained constant all these years. It is an outlook which also allows me to meet young people wherever I go. Every parish priest in Rome knows that my visits to the parish must conclude with a meeting between the Bishop of Rome and the young people of the parish. And not only in Rome, but anywhere the Pope goes, *he seeks out the young and the young seek him out. Actually, in truth, it is not the Pope who is being sought out at all. The one being sought out is Christ*, who knows "that which is in every man" (cf. Jn 2:25), especially in a young person, and who can give true answers to his questions! And even if they are demanding answers, the young are not afraid of them; more to the point, they even await them.

. . .

This also explains the idea of holding World Youth Days. At the very beginning, during the Jubilee Year of the Redemption, and then again for the International Year of Youth, sponsored by the United Nations (1985), young people were invited to Rome. This was the beginning. *No one invented the World Youth Days. It was the young people themselves who created them.* Those Days, those encounters, then became something desired by young people throughout the world. Most of the time these Days were something of a surprise for priests, and even bishops, in that they surpassed all their expectations.

The World Youth Days have become a great and fascinating witness that young people give of themselves. They have become a powerful means of evangelization. *In the young there is, in fact, an immense potential for good and for creative possibility.* Whenever I meet them in my travels throughout the world, I *wait first of all to hear what they want to tell me about themselves,* about their society, about their Church. And I always point out: "What I am going to say to you is not as important as what you are going to say to me. You will not necessarily say it to me in words; you will say it to me by your presence, by your song, perhaps by your dancing, by your skits, and finally by your enthusiasm."

We need the enthusiasm of the young. We need their *joie de vivre.* In it is reflected something of the original joy God had in creating man. The young experience this same joy within themselves. This joy is the same every-where, but it is also ever new and original. The young know how to express this joy in their own special way.

It is not true that the Pope brings the young from one end of the world to the other. It is they who bring him. Even though he is getting older, they urge him to be young, they do not permit him to forget his experience, his discovery of youth and its great importance for the life of every man. I believe this explains a great deal.

The very day of the inauguration of my papal ministry, on October 22, 1978, at the conclusion of the liturgy, I said to the young people gathered in St. Peter's Square: "You are the hope of the Church and of the world. You are my hope." I have often repeated these words.

I would like to sum up by stressing that *the young are searching for God,* they are searching for the meaning of life, they are searching for definitive answers: "What must I do to inherit eternal life?" (Lk 10:25). In this search, they cannot help but encounter the Church. *And the Church also cannot help but encounter the young.* The only necessity is that the Church have a profound understanding of what it means to be young, of the importance that youth has for every person. *It is also necessary that the young know the Church, that they perceive Christ in the Church,* Christ who walks through the centuries alongside each generation, alongside every person. He walks alongside each person as a friend. An important day in a young person's life is the day on which he becomes convinced that this is the only Friend who will not disappoint him, on whom he can always count.

Was God at Work in the Fall of Communism?

God seems to be silent (the "silence of God" as some have said and continue to say still), but in reality, He is constantly at work. Or so claim those who discern the unveiling of Providence's enigmatic plan in human affairs.

To remain within the context of recent events, Your Holiness has often expressed the personal conviction (I remember, for example, the words you spoke in the Baltic countries, during your first visit to ex-Soviet territory, in the autumn of 1993) that in the collapse of atheistic Marxism one can discern the *digitus Dei,* the "finger of God." You often have alluded to a "mystery," even a "miracle," when speaking of the collapse, after seventy years, of a power that seemed as if it would be around for centuries.

CHRIST SAYS: MY FATHER IS AT WORK UNTIL now, so I am at work" (Jn 5:17). What do these words refer to? Union with the Father, the Son, and the Holy Spirit is the essential constitutive element of eternal life. "This is eternal life, that they should know you . . . and the one whom you sent, Jesus Christ" (Jn 17:3). But when Jesus speaks of the Father who "is at work until now," He is not referring directly to eternity. He speaks of the fact that God is at work in the world. *Christianity is not only a religion of knowledge, of contemplation. It is a religion of God's action and of man's action.* That great master of mystical life and contemplation, Saint John of the Cross, has written: "At the evening of our life we will be judged on love" (*The Sayings of Light and Love* 60). Jesus expressed the same truth even more simply in speaking of the Last Judgment in the Gospel of Saint Matthew (25:31–46).

Can one speak of God's silence? And if so, how should one interpret such a silence?

Yes, in a certain sense God is silent, *because He has already revealed everything.* He spoke "in ancient times" through the Prophets and "in these last days" through His Son (cf. Heb 1:1–2). In the Son He said to us all that He had to say. Saint John of the Cross says that Christ is "like an abundant mine with many recesses of treasures, so that however deep individuals may go they never reach the end or bottom, but rather in every recess find new veins with new riches everywhere" (*Spiritual Canticle* 37.4). We need then to listen once more to the voice of God who speaks in human history. And if His word is not heard, perhaps it is because "the ears" of our hearts are not open to it. In this sense Christ spoke of those who "look but do not see and hear but do not listen or understand" (cf. Mt 13:13), while the experience of God is always within every man's reach, accessible to him in Jesus Christ and in the power of the Holy Spirit.

Today, despite how things might appear, there are many who find the way to experience *God who is at work*. This is powerfully experienced in our time, especially by the younger generation. What other interpretation could one give not only to all of the *associations*, but to the many *movements* flourishing in the Church? What else can these be, if not the word of God which has been heard and welcomed? And how else could the *experience of the World Youth Day in Denver* be understood, if not as the voice of God being heard by young people in a situation which, humanly speaking, offered no hope of success, also because much was being done to prevent that voice from being heard?

This hearing, this knowledge, is at the origin of action: it gives rise to the *movement of thought*, the *movement of the heart*, the *movement of the will*. I once said, to the leaders of apostolic movements, that *the Church itself is first and foremost a "movement," a mission*. It is the mission that begins in God the Father and that, through the Son in the Holy Spirit, continually reaches humanity and shapes it in a new way. Yes, Christianity is a great action of God. *The action of the word becomes the action of the sacraments.*

What else are the sacraments (all of them!), if not the action of Christ in the Holy Spirit? When the Church baptizes, it is Christ who baptizes; when the Church absolves, it is Christ who absolves; when the Church celebrates the Eucharist, it is Christ who celebrates it: "This is my body." And so on. All the sacraments are an action of Christ, the action of God in Christ. And therefore it is truly *difficult to speak of the silence of God.* One must speak, rather, of the desire to stifle the voice of God.

Yes, this *desire to stifle the voice of God* is rather carefully planned. Many will do just about anything so that His voice cannot be heard, so that only the voice of man will be heard, a voice that has nothing to offer except the things of this world. And sometimes such an offer brings with it destruction of cosmic proportions. Isn't this the tragic history of our century?

By your question you confirm that in *the fall of Communism* the action of God has become almost visible in the history of our century. We must be wary of over-simplification. What we refer to as Communism has its own history. It is the history of protest in the face of injustice, as I recalled in the encyclical *Laborem Exercens*—a protest on the part of the great world of workers, which then became an ideology. But *this protest has also become part of the teaching of the Church.* We need but recall the encyclical *Rerum Novarum,* from the end of the last century. We add: this teaching *is not limited to protest, but throws a far-seeing glance toward the future.* In fact, it was Leo XIII who in a certain sense predicted the fall of Communism, a fall which would cost humanity and Europe dearly, *since the medicine*—he wrote in his encyclical of 1891—*could prove more dangerous than the disease itself!* The Pope said this with all the seriousness and the authority of the Church's Magisterium.

And what are we to say of the *three children from Fátima* who suddenly, on the eve of the outbreak of the October Revolution, heard: "Russia will convert" and "In the end, my Heart will triumph" . . . ? They could not have invented those predictions. They did not know enough about history or geography, much less the social movements and ideological developments. And nevertheless it happened just as they had said.

Perhaps this is also why the Pope was called from "a faraway country," perhaps this is why it was necessary for the assassination attempt to be made in St. Peter's Square precisely on May 13, 1981, the anniversary of the first apparition at Fátima—so that all could become more transparent and comprehensible, so that the voice of God which speaks in human history through the "signs of the times" could be more easily heard and understood.

This, then, is the Father who is always at work, and this is the Son, who is also at work, and this is the invisible Holy Spirit who is Love, and as Love is ceaseless creative, saving, sanctifying, and life-giving action.

Therefore, it would be simplistic to say that Divine Providence caused the fall of Communism. In a certain sense Communism as a system fell by itself. It fell as a consequence of its own mistakes and abuses. *It proved to be a medicine more dangerous than the disease itself.* It did not bring about true social reform, yet it did become a powerful threat and challenge to the entire world. But *it fell by itself, because of its own inherent weakness.*

"My Father is at work until now, so I am at work" (Jn 5:17). The fall of Communism opens before us a *retrospective panorama of modern civilization's typical way of thinking and acting,* especially in Europe, where Communism originated. Modern civilization, despite undisputed successes in many fields, has also made many mistakes and given rise to many abuses with regard to man, exploiting him in various ways. It is a civilization that constantly equips itself with power structures and structures of oppression, both political and cultural (especially through the media), in order to impose similar mistakes and abuses on all humanity.

How else can we explain the increasing gap between the rich North and the ever poorer South? Who is responsible for this? Man is responsible—man, ideologies, and philosophical systems. I would say that *respon-sibility lies with the struggle against God, the systematic elimination of all that is Christian.* This struggle has to a large degree dominated thought and life in the West for three centuries. *Marxist collectivism is nothing more than a "cheap version" of this plan.* Today a similar plan is reveal-ing itself in all its danger and, at the same time, in all its faultiness.

God, on the other hand, is faithful to His Covenant. He has made it with humanity in Jesus Christ. He cannot now withdraw from it, having decided once and for all that the destiny of man is eternal life and the Kingdom of Heaven. *Will man surrender to the love of God, will he recognize his tragic mistake?* Will the Prince of Darkness surrender, he who is "the father of lies" (Jn 8:44), who continually accuses the sons of men as once he accused Job (cf. Jb 1:9ff)? It is unlikely that he will surrender, but his arguments may weaken. Perhaps, little by little, humanity will become more sober, people will open their ears once more in order to hear that word by which God has said everything to humanity.

And there will be nothing humiliating about this. Every person can learn from his own mistakes. So can humanity, allowing God to lead the way along the wind-ing paths of history. God does not cease to be at work. *His essential work will always remain the Cross and the Res-urrection of Christ.* This is the ultimate word of truth and of love. This is also the unending source of God's action in the sacraments, as well as in other ways that are known to Him alone. His is an action which passes through the heart of man and through the history of humanity.

Is Only Rome Right?

Let's return to those three realities of the Catholic faith, inseparable from one another, of which we spoke earlier. We have already spoken of God and Jesus Christ. It's time to talk about the Church.

It has been observed that the majority of people, even in the West, still believe in God (or at least "some God"). Declared atheism has always been—and seems to continue to be—confined to the *elite* and intellectuals. The belief that God "became incarnate" Himself—or at least uniquely "manifested" Himself—in Jesus is still held by many.

But the Church? The Catholic Church, in particular? Today many people seem to rebel against the claim that salvation can be found only in the Church. Many Christians—and even some Catholics—ask themselves: Why, among all the Christian Churches, should the Catholic Church alone possess and teach the fullness of the Gospel?

HERE, BEFORE ALL ELSE, WE NEED TO EXPLAIN the *Christian doctrine of salvation and of the mediation of salvation,* which always originates in God. "For there is one God. / There is also one mediator between God and the human race, / Christ Jesus, himself human" (1 Tm 2:5). "There is no salvation through . . . any other name" (Acts 4:12).

It is therefore a revealed truth that *there is salvation only and exclusively in Christ.* The Church, inasmuch as it is the Body of Christ, is simply an instrument of this salvation. In the first words of *Lumen Gentium,* the Dogmatic Constitution on the Church of the Second Vatican Council, we read: "The Church is in Christ as a sacrament, or a sign and instrument, of intimate union with God and of the unity of the entire human race" (*Lumen Gentium* 1). As the people of God the Church is thus, at the same time, the Body of Christ.

The Council explained in great depth the *mystery of the Church:* "The Son of God, uniting Himself to human nature and conquering death with His Death and Resurrection, redeemed man and transformed him into a new creation (cf. Gal 6:15; 2 Cor 5:17). By sending forth His Spirit Christ calls together His brothers from among all peoples to form His mystical body" (*Lumen Gentium* 7). For this reason, as Saint Cyprian says, the universal Church appears as "a people gathered together by the unity of the Father, the Son, and the Holy Spirit" (*De Oratione Dominica* 23). This life, which is life from God and in God, is the actualization of salvation. *Man is saved in the Church by being brought into the Mystery of the Divine Trinity,* into the mystery of the intimate life of God.

This cannot be understood by looking exclusively at the visible aspect of the Church. The Church is a *living body.* Saint Paul expressed this in his brilliant insights about the Body of Christ (cf. Col 1:18).

"In this way we all become members of that Body (cf. 1 Cor 12:27), and 'individually members of one another' (Rm 12:5). . . . There is also a diversity of parts and functions in the structure of the mystical Body. One is the Spirit, who for the good of the Church distributes His various gifts with a magnificence equal to His richness and to the needs of the ministries" (*Lumen Gentium* 7).

Thus, the Council is far from proclaiming any kind of *ecclesiocentrism.* Its teaching is *Christocentric* in all of its aspects, and therefore it is profoundly rooted in the Mystery of the Trinity. At the heart of the Church is Christ and His Sacrifice, a Sacrifice celebrated in a certain sense on the altar of all creation, on the altar of the world. Christ "is . . . / the firstborn of all creation" (Col 1:15); through His Resurrection He is also "the firstborn from the dead" (Col 1:18). Around His redemptive sacrifice is gathered all creation, which is working out its eternal destiny in God. If this process causes pain, it is, however, full of hope, as Saint Paul teaches in the Letter to the Romans (cf. Rom 8:23–24).

. . .

"The one People of God is present among all nations on earth, since he takes its citizens from every race, citizens of a Kingdom that by its nature is not of this world but from heaven. In fact all of the faithful spread throughout the world are in communion with one another through the Holy Spirit, and so 'he who is in Rome knows that those on the far side of the earth are his members.'" In the same document, one of the most important of the Second Vatican Council, we read: "In virtue of this catholicity, each individual part brings its gifts to the other parts and to the entire Church, and thus the whole and individual parts are reinforced by communicating with each other, working together to attain fulfillment in unity" (*Lumen Gentium* 13).

In Christ the Church is a communion in many different ways. Its character as a communion renders the Church similar to the communion of the Divine Trinity of the Father and the Son and the Holy Spirit. Thanks to this communion, the Church is the instrument of man's salvation. It both contains and continually draws upon the mystery of Christ's redemptive sacrifice. Through the shedding of His own blood, Jesus Christ constantly "enters into God's sanctuary thus obtaining eternal redemption" (cf. Heb 9:12).

Thus, Christ is the true active subject of humanity's salvation. The Church is as well, inasmuch as it acts on behalf of Christ and in Christ. As the Council teaches:

"Christ, present among us in His Body which is the Church, is the one mediator and the way to salvation. Expressly asserting the need for faith and baptism (cf. Mk 16:16; Jn 3:5), he asserted the need for the Church, which men enter through baptism as if through a door. For this reason men cannot be saved who do not want to enter or remain in the Church, knowing that the Catholic Church was founded by God through Christ as a necessity" (*Lumen Gentium* 14).

Here the Council sets forth its teaching on the Church as *the active subject of salvation in Christ*: "Fully incorporated into the society of the Church are those who, having the Spirit of Christ, integrally accept its organization and all means of salvation instituted in it. In the Church's visible structure they are joined with Christ—who rules the Church through the Supreme Pontiff and the bishops—by the bonds of the profession of the faith, the sacraments, ecclesiastical government, and Communion. Those who do not persist in charity, even if they remain in the Church in 'body' but not in 'heart,' cannot be saved. All of the Church's children must remember that their privileged condition is not the result of their own merits, but the result of the special grace of Christ. Therefore, if someone does not respond to this grace in thought, in word, and in deeds, not only will that person not be saved, he will be even more severely judged" (*Lumen Gentium* 14). I think that the Council's words fully respond to the difficulty raised by your question; they shed light on *why the Church is necessary for salvation*.

The Council speaks of *membership in the Church* for Christians and of *being related to the Church* for non-Christian believers in God, for people of goodwill (cf. *Lumen Gentium* 15–16). Both these dimensions are important for salvation, and each one possesses varying levels. People are saved *through* the Church, they are saved *in* the Church, but they always are saved *by the grace of Christ*. Besides formal membership in the Church, *the sphere of salvation* can also include *other forms of relation to the Church*. Paul VI expressed this same teaching in his first encyclical, *Ecclesiam Suam*, when he spoke of the various *circles of the dialogue of salvation* (cf. *Ecclesiam Suam* 101–117), which are the same as those indicated by the Council as the spheres of membership in and of relation to the Church. This is the authentic meaning of the well-known statement "Outside the Church there is no salvation."

It would be difficult to deny that this doctrine is extremely *open*. It cannot be accused of an *ecclesiological exclusivism*. Those who rebel against claims allegedly made by the Catholic Church probably do not have an adequate understanding of this teaching.

Although the Catholic Church knows that it has received *the fullness of the means of salvation*, it rejoices when other Christian communities join her in preaching the Gospel. *This is the proper context for understanding the Council's teaching that the Church of Christ "subsists" in the Catholic Church* (cf. *Lumen Gentium* 8; *Unitatis Redintegratio* 4).

The Church, precisely because it is Catholic, is open to dialogue with all other Christians, with the followers of non-Christian religions, and also with all people of good will, as John XXIII and Paul VI frequently said. *Lumen Gentium* explains convincingly and in depth the meaning of "people of good will." The Church wants to preach the Gospel *together with all who believe in Christ.* It wants to point out to all the path to eternal salvation, the fundamental principles of life in the Spirit and in truth.

Permit me to recall the years of my early youth. I remember that one day my father gave me a prayerbook which contained the *prayer to the Holy Spirit.* He told me to recite it daily. So, from that day on, I have tried to. I understood for the first time the meaning of Christ's words to the Samaritan woman about the true worshipers of God, about those who worship Him in Spirit and truth (cf. Jn 4:23). There were to be many more steps in my journey. Before entering the seminary, I met a layman named *Jan Tyranowski,* who was a true mystic. This man, whom I consider a saint, introduced me to the great Spanish mystics and in particular to Saint John of the Cross. Even before entering the underground seminary, I read the works of that mystic, especially his poetry. In order to read it in the original, I studied Spanish. That was a very important stage in my life.

I think, however, that here *my father's words played a very important role because they directed me toward becom-*

ing a true worshiper of God—they directed me toward trying to be one of His true worshipers, of those who worship Him in Spirit and truth. I discovered the Church to be a community of salvation. In this Church I found my place and my vocation. Gradually, I learned the meaning of the redemption accomplished in Christ and, as a result, the meaning of the sacraments, and of Holy Mass in particular. I learned at what price we have been redeemed. And all of this drew me even more profoundly into the mystery of the Church, which, precisely because it is a mystery, has an invisible dimension. The Council spoke of this as well. *This mystery is larger than the visible structure and organization of the Church.* Structure and organization are at the service of the mystery. The Church, as the mystical Body of Christ, penetrates and embraces all of us. *The spiritual, mystical dimensions of the Church are much greater than any sociological statistics could ever possibly show.*

In Search of
Lost Unity

YOUR LAST RESPONSE RAISES ANOTHER QUES-
tion. In addition to having undeniably positive
results, ecumenical dialogue—the endeavor to reunite all
Christians in accordance with the prayers of Christ Himself—seems to have had its share of disappointments.
Recently, for example, certain decisions made by the
Anglican Church have created new obstacles just when
there seemed to be hope of closer union. Your Holiness,
with regard to this crucial issue, what are your impres-
sions and your hopes?

BEFORE SPEAKING ABOUT DISAPPOINTMENTS
it is appropriate to speak briefly on the Second
Vatican Council's initiative once more to set the Church
on the path of ecumenism. This path is very dear to me.
I come from a country of deeply rooted *ecumenical tra-*

ditions, despite its reputation for being predominantly Catholic.

In the course of its millennial history, Poland has been a state made up of many nationalities, many religions—mostly Christian, but not only Christian. This tradition has been and still is the source of a positive aspect of Polish culture, namely its *tolerance* and *openness* toward people who think differently, who speak other languages, or who believe, pray, or celebrate the same mysteries of faith in a different way. Nevertheless, throughout the history of Poland there have been concrete *efforts to bring about unity.* The Union of Brest-Litovsk in 1596 marks the beginning of the history of the Eastern Church. Today this church is called the Catholic Church of the Byzantine-Ukrainian Rite, but at that time it was mainly the Church of the Russian and Byelorussian people.

This is meant to be a kind of introduction to my response to the opinions of some people with regard to the *disappointment experienced in the ecumenical dialogue.* I think that more powerful than these disappointments is the very fact that the path to Christian unity has been undertaken with renewed vigor. As we near the end of the second millennium, Christians are more deeply aware that the divisions existing between them are contrary to Christ's prayer at the Last Supper: "that they may all be one, as you, Father, are in me and I in you . . . that the world may believe that you sent me" (cf. Jn 17:21).

Christians of different denominations and communities have been able to appreciate the truth of these words especially as a result of *missionary activity*, which has recently intensified, both on the part of the Catholic Church, as I noted earlier, and on the part of different Protestant Churches and communities. The people to whom missionaries proclaim Christ and His Gospel, preaching ideals of fraternity and unity, cannot help but ask questions about the unity of Christians. And they need to know which of these Churches or communities is that of Christ, since He founded only one Church—the only one capable of speaking in His name. Therefore, in a certain sense the experience of missionary activity gave rise to today's ecumenical movement.

Pope John XXIII, who was moved by God to summon the Council, used to say: "What separates us as believers in Christ is much less than what unites us." In this statement we find the *heart of ecumenical thinking*. The Second Vatican Council continued in the same direction, as we have seen in passages already cited from the Dogmatic Constitution on the Church, to which we should also add the Decree on Ecumenism, *Unitatis Redintegratio*, and the Declaration on Religious Liberty, *Dignitatis Humanae*. These last two documents are extremely important from an ecumenical point of view.

What unites us is much greater than what separates us: the Council documents gave a more concrete form to John XXIII's fundamental intuition. All of us, in fact, believe in the same Christ. This faith is the fundamental inheritance of the teaching of the first seven ecumenical councils, which were held in the first millennium. So there is basis for dialogue and *for the growth of unity,* a growth that should occur at the same rate at which we are able to overcome our divisions—divisions that to a great degree result from the idea that one can have a monopoly on truth.

These divisions are certainly opposed to what Christ had in mind. It is impossible to imagine that this Church, instituted by Christ on the foundation of the apostles and of Peter, should not be one. But we can also understand how over the centuries contact with different political and cultural climates could have led believers to interpret Christ's message with varying emphases.

Nevertheless, *these different approaches to understanding and living out one's faith in Christ can, in certain cases, be complementary;* they do not have to be mutually exclusive. Good will is needed in order to realize how various interpretations and ways of practicing the faith can come together and complement each other. There is also the need to determine *where genuine divisions start, the point beyond which the faith is compromised.* It is legitimate to affirm that the gap between the Catholic and the Orthodox Church is not very wide. On the other hand, with regard to the Churches and the communities originating in the Reformation, we must recognize that the gap is considerably wider, since several fundamental elements established by Christ were not respected.

At the same time, we must also acknowledge that difficulties of a *psychological and historical nature* are at times felt more deeply in the Orthodox Churches than in some Protestant communities. This is why personal contacts are so important. I grow more convinced of this every time I meet leaders of these Churches, whether in Rome or during visits to various parts of the world. The very fact that we are able to come together and pray is very significant. Some years ago this was absolutely unthinkable.

In this regard, I must mention several visits I made that had particular importance from an ecumenical point of view—for example, those to Great Britain and to Scandinavia. In general, we can observe that *subjective difficulties are greater in those countries where the division first arose.* Therefore, with regard to Protestantism, these difficulties are felt far more in Germany and in Switzerland than, for example, in North America or in Africa. I will never forget the statement I heard during an ecumenical gathering with representatives of the Protestant community in Cameroon: "We know we are divided, but we do not know why."

In Europe the situation is quite different. Nevertheless, one can see much evidence of a growing desire to work for Christian unity.

. . .

Clearly, the disappointments to which you referred were bound to arise in the case of individuals or groups that viewed the problem of Christian unity in too casual and superficial a way. Many enthusiastic people, sustained by great optimism, were ready to believe that the Second Vatican Council had already resolved the problem. But the Council only opened the road to unity, committing first of all the Catholic Church; but *that road itself is a process,* which must gradually overcome many obstacles—whether of a doctrinal or a cultural or a social nature—that have accumulated over the course of centuries. It is necessary, therefore, *to rid ourselves of stereotypes, of old habits.* And above all, it is necessary *to recognize the unity that already exists.*

Much has been accomplished along these lines. At various levels the ecumenical dialogue continues to develop and is bearing much good fruit. A number of theological commissions are going about their work in a spirit of cooperation. Anyone who follows these matters closely cannot help but sense the presence of the Holy Spirit. However, no one really believes that the way toward unity is short or free of obstacles. Above all else, *much prayer* is needed, as well as great commitment to the task of profound conversion, which can only be brought about by common prayer and joint efforts on behalf of justice, peace, and the shaping of the temporal order ever more fully in accordance with Christian values, on behalf of everything that the mission of Christians in the world demands.

In our century in particular, events have taken place that clash profoundly with the truth of the Gospel. I allude above all to the *two World Wars* and to the concentration and extermination camps. Paradoxically, these events may have reinforced ecumenical consciousness among divided Christians. In this regard, the *extermination of the Jews* certainly had a special role. It placed before both the Church and Christianity the issue of the relationship between the Old and the New Testaments. The Second Vatican Council's Declaration *Nostra Aetate* is the result of the Catholic Church's reflections on this relationship. The Council contributed greatly to the development of the awareness that the children of Israel are our "elder brothers." This development was the result of dialogue, ecumenical dialogue in particular. In the Catholic Church it is significant that dialogue with the Jews takes place in the Pontifical Council for Promoting Christian Unity, which is also concerned with the dialogue among the various Christian communities.

Taking all this into consideration, it is difficult not to acknowledge that the Catholic Church has enthusiastically embraced ecumenism in all its complexity and carries it out day after day with great seriousness. Naturally, real unity is not and cannot be the fruit of human forces alone. *The true protagonist remains the Holy Spirit,* who must determine, even from the human point of view, when the process of unity has developed sufficiently.

When will this happen? It is not easy to predict. In any case, in light of the coming of the third millennium, Christians have noted that while the Church was undivided during the first millennium, the second was marked by many profound divisions to the East and West, which today need to be mended.

By the year 2000 we need to be more united, more willing to advance along the path toward the unity for which Christ prayed on the eve of His Passion. This unity is enormously precious. In a certain sense, the future of the world is at stake. The future of the Kingdom of God in the world is at stake. Human weaknesses and prejudices cannot destroy God's plan for the world and for humanity. If we appreciate this, we can look to the future with a certain *optimism*. We can trust that "the one who began this good work in us will bring it to completion" (cf. Phil 1:6).

WHY DIVIDED?

GOD'S PLANS ARE OFTEN INSCRUTABLE. Only in the hereafter will it be truly possible to "see" and, therefore, to understand. But would it be possible to have a glimpse even now of the answer to the question that, for centuries, many believers have asked? Why would the Holy Spirit have permitted so many different divisions and enmities among those who claim to be disciples of the same Gospel, disciples of the same Christ?

YES, INDEED, WE CAN TRULY ASK OURSELVES: *Why did the Holy Spirit permit all these divisions?* In general, the causes and historical development of these divisions are well known. It is legitimate, however, to wonder if there is perhaps a *metahistorical reason as well.*

There are two possible answers to this question. The more *negative* one would see in these divisions the bitter fruit of sins committed by Christians. The more positive answer is inspired by trust in the One who is capable of bringing forth good even from evil, from human weakness. Could it not be that these divisions have also been *a path continually leading the Church to discover the untold wealth contained in Christ's Gospel and in the redemption accomplished by Christ?* Perhaps all this wealth would not have come to light otherwise. . . .

More generally, we can affirm that for human knowledge and human action a certain *dialectic* is present. Didn't the Holy Spirit, in His divine "condescendence," take this into consideration? It is necessary *for humanity to achieve unity through plurality, to learn to come together in the one Church, even while presenting a plurality of ways of thinking and acting, of cultures and civilizations.* Wouldn't such a way of looking at things be, in a certain sense, more consonant with the wisdom of God, with His goodness and providence?

Nevertheless, this cannot be a justification for the divisions that continue to deepen! *The time must come for the love that unites us to be manifested!* Many things lead us to believe that that time is now here, and as a result, the importance of ecumenism for Christianity should be evident. Ecumenism is a response to the exhortation in the First Letter of Peter to "give an explanation [of] the reason for our hope" (cf. 1 Pt 3:15).

Mutual respect is a prerequisite for authentic ecumenism. Earlier, in recalling my experiences in my homeland, I pointed out the historical events that shaped Poland as a society characterized by a broad tolerance for many beliefs and many nationalities. At a time in Western history when heretics were being tried and burned at the stake, the last Polish king of the Jagiellon dynasty gave proof of this with the words "I am not the king of your consciences."

Let's remember for that matter that the Lord Jesus conferred upon Peter certain pastoral duties, which consist in preserving the unity of the flock. The *Petrine ministry* is also a *ministry of unity,* which is carried out in the field of ecumenism. Peter's task is to search constantly for ways that will help preserve unity. Therefore he must not create obstacles but must open up paths. Nor is this in any way at odds with the duty entrusted to him by Christ: "strengthen your brothers in faith" (cf. Lk 22:32). It is significant that Christ said these words precisely at the moment when Peter was about to deny Him. It was as if the Master Himself wanted to tell Peter: "Remember that you are weak, that you, too, need endless conversion. *You are able to strengthen others only insofar as you are aware of your own weakness.* I entrust to you as your responsibility the truth, the great truth of God, meant for man's salvation, but this truth cannot be preached or put into practice except by loving." *Veritatem facere in caritate* (To live the truth in love; cf. Eph 4:15); this is what is always necessary.

The Church
and the Council

ALLOW ME TO PLAY, ALTHOUGH RESPECT-fully, the gadfly, to speak on behalf of all those who reject both optimism and pessimism in order to stick to cold realism. You are certainly aware that there has not been, nor is there presently, a lack of people who claim that if we take a close look at the years which followed the Second Vatican Council, the doors which the Council threw open ended up allowing those who were "inside" the Church to exit, rather than for those who were "outside" to enter. There are those who do not hesitate to voice concern about the situation of the Church, claiming that its unity of faith and government is not as strong as it was, but rather, is threatened by divisive forces.

ALLOW ME ONCE MORE TO DISAGREE WITH such a way of looking at things. What I have said up to this point leads me to have, regarding this issue, a different opinion from the people you mention. My opinion is based on faith in the Holy Spirit who guides the Church, and also from a careful observation of the facts. *The Second Vatican Council was a great gift to the Church,* to all those who took part in it, to the entire human family, and to each of us individually.

It is difficult to say something new about the Second Vatican Council. At the same time, we must always refer back to the Council, which is a duty and a challenge for the Church and for the world. We feel the need to speak about the Council *in order to interpret it correctly and defend it from tendentious interpretations.* Such interpretations do in fact exist and they did not appear only at the end of the Council. In a certain sense the Council already found them in the world and even in the Church. These interpretations were an expression of *outlooks, either favorable or opposed to accepting and understanding the Council,* as well as committing oneself to making it a part of one's life.

I had the particular fortune of *being able to take part in the Council from the first day to the last.* This was in no way to be taken for granted, since the Communist authorities in my country considered the trip to Rome a privilege and entirely under their control. If, then, under such circumstances I was given the opportunity to participate in the Council from the beginning to the end, it can rightly be judged a *special gift from God*.

On the basis of my experience at the Council I wrote *Sources of Renewal*. At the beginning of the book, I stated that the book was an *attempt to repay the debt* to the Holy Spirit incurred by every bishop who participated in the Council. Yes, the Council contained something of Pentecost—it set the bishops of the world, and hence the whole Church, upon the paths that needed to be taken at the end of the second millennium. Paul VI spoke of these paths in the encyclical *Ecclesiam Suam* (cf. 60 ff).

At the beginning of my participation in the Council, I was a young bishop. I remember that at first my seat was right next to the entrance of St. Peter's Basilica. From the third session on—after I was appointed Archbishop of Kraków—I was moved closer to the altar.

The Council was a unique occasion for listening to others, but also for creative thinking. Naturally, the older and more expert bishops contributed the most to the development of the Council's thought. At first, since I was young, I learned more than I contributed. Gradually, however, I came to participate in the Council in a more mature and creative manner.

Thus, by the third session *I found myself a member of the group preparing the so-called Thirteenth Schema*, the document that would become the Pastoral Constitution

Gaudium et Spes. I was able to participate in the extremely interesting work of this group which was made up of representatives of the Theological Commission and of the lay apostolate. I will never forget the meeting at Ariccia in January 1965. I am personally indebted to Cardinal Gabriel-Marie Garrone for his fundamental help in drafting the new document. The same is true for the other bishops and theologians with whom I had the good fortune to work. I am particularly indebted to Father Yves Congar and to Father Henri De Lubac. I still remember today the words with which the latter encouraged me to persevere in the line of thought that I had taken up during the discussion. This happened when the meetings were taking place at the Vatican. From that moment on I enjoyed a special friendship with Father De Lubac.

The Council was a *great experience of the Church;* it was—as we said at the time—*the "seminary of the Holy Spirit."* At the Council the Holy Spirit spoke to the Church in all its universality, which was reflected in the presence of bishops from the whole world and by the presence of representatives of many non-Catholic Churches and communities.

The words of the Holy Spirit always represent a deeper insight into the eternal mystery, and point out the paths to be walked by those entrusted with the task of bringing this mystery to the contemporary world. Even the fact that those men were called together by the Holy Spirit and formed, during the Council, a special community that listened together, prayed together, thought and created together, has a fundamental importance for evangelization, for the *new evangelization, which originated precisely at the Second Vatican Council.* All of this is closely linked to a new era in the history of humanity and in the history of the Church.

A "Dialogue of Salvation"

The Holy Father has no doubt: In that period of the history of the Church and of the world, there was need for an ecumenical council like the Second Vatican Council, "anomalous" in style and content with respect to the other preceding twenty Councils, from Nicaea in 325 to the First Vatican Council in 1869.

———

There was need of a council not so much to oppose a particular heresy, as was the case in the early centuries, but rather to set in motion a sort of *double process:* on the one hand, overcoming the divisions in Christianity which had multiplied throughout the second millennium; on the other, reviving, as much as possible in common, the preaching of the Gospel on the threshold of the third millennium.

In light of this, as you rightly observe, the Second Vatican Council differed from earlier councils because of *its particular style.* It was not a defensive style. Not once in the Council documents do the words *anathema sit* appear. It was an *ecumenical style,* characterized by great openness to dialogue, a dialogue described by Pope Paul VI as a "dialogue of salvation."

This dialogue was not intended to be limited to Christians alone. It was meant to be open to non-Christian religions, and to reach the whole modern world, including those who do not believe. *Truth, in fact, cannot be confined.* Truth is for one and for all. And if this truth comes about through love (cf. Eph 4:15), then it becomes even more universal. This was the style of the Second Vatican Council and the spirit in which it took place.

This style and this spirit will be remembered as the essential truth about the Council, not the controversies between "liberals" and "conservatives"—controversies seen in political, not religious, terms—to which some people wanted to reduce the whole Council. In this spirit the Second Vatican Council will continue to be a challenge for all Churches and a duty for each person for a long time to come.

In the decades that have passed since the conclusion of the Second Vatican Council, we have been able to see how this challenge and this duty have been received under various conditions and at various levels. We saw this first with the *post-conciliar synods*—whether the general Synods of Bishops from all over the world convened by the Pope, or those of the individual dioceses or ecclesiastical provinces. I know from experience how this *synodal approach* responds to expectations of various groups and what it can achieve. I think of the diocesan synods which almost spontaneously got rid of the old unilateral emphasis on clergy and became *a means for expressing the responsibility of each person toward the Church*. The sense of communal responsibility toward the Church, felt especially by lay people today, is certainly a source of renewal. In view of the third millennium, this sense of responsibility will shape the image of the Church for generations to come.

In 1985, the twentieth anniversary of the Council's closing, an extraordinary Synod of Bishops was convened. I bring this up because from that Synod came the idea of the *Catechism of the Catholic Church*. Some theologians, at times whole groups, spread the notion that there was no longer a need for a catechism, that it was an obsolete means of handing down the faith, and therefore should be abandoned. They also expressed the opinion that it would be impossible to create a catechism for the universal Church. These were the same groups that had earlier judged the Code of Canon Law, already called for by John XXIII, as useless and inappropriate. But the voice of the bishops assembled at the Synod painted an entirely different picture—the new

Code had been a timely initiative which met a need within the Church.

The Catechism was also indispensable, *in order that all the richness of the teaching of the Church following the Second Vatican Council could be preserved in a new synthesis and be given a new direction.* Without the Catechism of the universal Church, this would not have been accomplished. On the basis of this text of the Church's Magisterium, individual groups could then go on to create their own catechisms according to local needs. In a relatively brief time the great synthesis was completed. The entire Church truly had a role in this. Cardinal Joseph Ratzinger, Prefect of the Congregation for the Doctrine of the Faith, deserves particular credit in this regard. The Catechism, published in 1992, became a best-seller worldwide, proving the great demand for this type of text, which at first glance might seem to be of limited interest only.

And interest in the Catechism continues. We find ourselves faced with a new reality. *The world, tired of ideology, is opening itself to the truth.* The time has come when the splendor of this truth (*veritatis splendor*) has begun anew to illuminate the darkness of human existence. Even if it is too early to judge, if we consider how much has been accomplished and how much is being accomplished, it is clear that *the Council will not remain a dead letter.*

The Spirit who spoke through the Second Vatican Council did not speak in vain. The experience of these years allows us to glimpse the possibility of a new openness toward God's truth, a truth the Church must preach "in season and out of season" (cf. 2 Tm 4:2). Every minister of the Gospel must be thankful and feel constantly indebted to the Holy Spirit for the gift of the Council. It will take many years and many generations to pay off this debt.

A QUALITATIVE
RENEWAL

ALLOW ME TO OBSERVE THAT YOUR VERY
clear words once again demonstrate the partiality,
the short-sightedness of those who have suspected you
of pushing for a "restoration," of being a "reactionary"
with regard to the Council.

Nevertheless, you are aware that only a few have gone
so far as to question whether there was a need for the
changes that took place in the Church. For others, the
Second Vatican Council itself is not the problem, but
rather certain interpretations of it which are not in line
with the spirit of the Council Fathers.

LET ME GO BACK TO AN EARLIER QUESTION,
which is, like certain other ones, intentionally
provocative. Did the Council throw open the doors so
that people today could enter the Church, or were the

doors opened so that individuals and groups could begin to leave the Church?

To a certain extent, the opinion you have expressed reflects a truth, especially if we look at the *Church in western Europe* (even if in western Europe we are now witnessing many signs of religious renewal). But the situation of the Church has to be looked at from a global perspective. We must take into consideration all *that is happening in central and eastern Europe and outside of Europe,* in North and South America, as well as in mission countries, in particular in Africa, in the vast areas of the Indian and Pacific Oceans, and, to a certain degree, even in the countries of Asia, including China. In many of those countries the Church has been built on the witness of martyrs, and on this foundation the Church is growing with ever increasing vigor—as a minority Church, yes, but one that is very much alive.

Since the Council, we have been witnessing *a primarily qualitative renewal.* Although priests continue to be scarce and the vocations are still too few, *religious movements are being born and are flourishing.* They arise from a background which is somewhat different from the older Catholic associations, which were more social in nature. These had been inspired by the Church's social doctrine and aimed at the transformation of society, at the establishment of social justice. Several of these movements entered so intensely into dialogue with Marxism that they lost to some degree their Catholic identity.

The new movements, instead, are oriented, before all else, toward the renewal of the individual. Man is the first agent of all social and historical change, but to be able to carry out this role he himself must be renewed in Christ, in the Holy Spirit. This is a direction which holds great promise for the future of the Church. *At one time the renewal of the Church took place mainly through the religious orders.* This was true in the period following the fall of the Roman Empire with the Benedictines and, in the Middle Ages, with the mendicant orders—the Franciscans and the Dominicans. This was true in the period following the Reformation, with the Jesuits and other similar congregations; in the eighteenth century, with the Redemptorists and the Passionists; in the nineteenth century, with dynamic missionary congregations such as the Divine Word Fathers, the Salvatorians, and, naturally, the Salesians.

Alongside the Religious Congregations of more recent origin, and the marvelous flowering of secular institutes during this century, the years during and following the Council witnessed the birth of these new movements. Also including consecrated religious, these movements are made up for the most part of lay people who are married and have professions. The ideal of the world's renewal in Christ springs directly from the fundamental duty of baptism.

It would be wrong, today, to speak only of people leaving the Church. There are also people who come back. *Above all, there has been a very radical transformation of our underlying model.* I have in mind Europe and America, in particular North America and, in another sense, South America. *The traditional quantitative model has been transformed into a new, more qualitative model.* This also is a result of the Council.

The Second Vatican Council appeared at the moment in which the old model was beginning to cede its place to the new. Therefore we have to say that *the Council came at the right time* and set about a task that was necessary not only for the Church, but for the entire world.

If the post-conciliar Church has difficulties in the area of doctrine and discipline, these difficulties are not serious enough to present a real threat of new divisions. The Church of the Second Vatican Council, *the Church marked by an intense collegiality among the world's bishops,* truly serves this world in a variety of ways and presents itself as the true Body of Christ, as the minister of His saving and redemptive mission, as the promoter of justice and peace. In a divided world, *the unity of the Catholic Church, which transcends national boundaries, remains a great force,* acknowledged as such even by its enemies and still present today in world politics and international organizations. Not everyone is comfortable with this force, but the Church continues to repeat with the Apostles: "It is impossible for us not to speak about what we have seen and heard" (cf. Acts 4:20). In this way, it remains faithful to itself and radiates that *veritatis splendor* which the Holy Spirit pours out upon His bride.

THE REACTION
OF THE "WORLD"

YOUR REFERENCE TO THE STEADFASTNESS OF Peter and John in the Acts of the Apostles—"It is impossible for us not to speak about what we have seen and heard" (Acts 4:20)—reminds us that, despite the Church's desire for dialogue, the words of the Pope are not always accepted by everyone. In more than a few cases they are explicitly rejected (if we are to believe the reports, not always accurate, carried throughout the world by the news media), especially when the Church reaffirms its teaching, particularly on certain moral issues.

———

YOU ALLUDE TO THE PROBLEM OF THE *reception of the Church's teaching in today's world,* especially in the area of ethics and morals. Some maintain that as far as issues of morality, and above all sexual ethics, are concerned, the Church and the Pope are not in touch with the contemporary world with its trends toward an ever greater freedom of conduct. Since the world is going in this direction, one gets the impression that the Church is moving backward, or, in any event, that the world is leaving the Church behind. The world, then, is moving away from the Pope; the world is moving away from the Church. . . .

This opinion is widespread, but I am convinced that it is quite wrong. The encyclical *Veritatis Splendor* demonstrates this, even if it does not directly address sexual ethics, but addresses rather the great threat posed to Western civilization by *moral relativism*. Pope Paul VI sensed this deeply and knew that it was his duty to undertake the battle against such relativism for the sake of the essential good of man. With his encyclical *Humanae Vitae* he put into practice the words the Apostle Paul wrote to his disciple Timothy: "Proclaim the word; be persistent whether it is convenient or inconvenient. . . . For the time will come when people will not tolerate sound doctrine" (2 Tm 4:2–3). Unfortunately, don't these words of the apostle seem to characterize the situation today?

The media have conditioned society to listen to what it wants to hear (cf. 2 Tm 4:3). An even worse situation occurs when theologians, and especially moralists, ally themselves with the media, which obviously pay a great deal of attention to what they have to say when it opposes "sound doctrine." Indeed, *when the true doctrine is unpopular, it is not right to seek easy popularity.* The

Church must give an honest answer to the question "What good must I do to gain eternal life?" (Mt 19:16). Christ forewarned us, telling us that the road to eternal salvation is not broad and comfortable, but narrow and difficult (cf. Mt 7:13–14). We do not have the right to abandon that perspective, nor to change it. This is what the Magisterium admonishes; it is also the duty of theologians—above all, moralists—who, in cooperation with the Magisterium, have their own special part to play.

Naturally, the words of Christ remain true when He warns about those burdens which certain teachers, unwilling themselves to carry them, load upon others (cf. Lk 11:46). But we have to consider *which is the greater burden—the truth, even the most demanding truth, or, instead, an appearance of truth, which creates only the illusion of moral honesty.* The encyclical *Veritatis Splendor* helps us to face this fundamental dilemma which people seem to be recognizing. I think, in fact, that today this dilemma is better understood than in 1968, when Paul VI published the encyclical *Humanae Vitae.*

Is it true that the Church has come to a standstill and that the world is moving away from it? Can we say that the world is only growing toward a greater freedom of behavior? Don't these words perhaps hide that relativism which is so detrimental to man? Not only abortion, but also contraception, *are ultimately bound up with the truth about man.* Moving away from this truth does not represent a step forward, and cannot be considered a measure of "ethical progress." Faced with similar trends, every pastor of the Church and, above all, the Pope must be particularly attentive so as not to ignore the strong warning contained in Paul's Second Letter to Timothy: "But you, be self-possessed in all circumstances; put up with hardship; perform the work of an evangelist; fulfill your ministry" (2 Tm 4:5).

Faith in the Church today. In the Creed—both in the Apostles' Creed and in the Nicene-Constantinopolitan Creed—we say: *I believe in the Church.* We place the Church on the same level as the Mystery of the Holy Trinity and the mysteries of the Incarnation and of the Redemption. Nevertheless, as Father De Lubac has clearly pointed out, this faith in the Church signifies something different from faith in the great mysteries of God Himself, since *we not only believe in the Church but at the same time we are the Church.* Following the Council, we can say that we believe in the Church as in a mystery. And at the same time, we know that as the people of God we are the Church. We are also the Church as people who belong to its visible structure and, above all, as sharers in Christ's messianic mission, which has a threefold character—prophetic, priestly, and kingly.

We can say that *our faith in the Church has been renewed and deepened in a significant way by the Council.* For a long time the Church paid more attention to its institutional and hierarchical dimension and neglected somewhat its fundamental dimension of grace and charism, which is proper to the people of God.

Thanks to the Council's teaching, we can say that *faith in the Church has been entrusted to us once again as a duty*. Post-conciliar renewal is above all a renewal of this extraordinarily rich and fruitful faith. Faith in the Church, as the Second Vatican Council teaches, demands that we reexamine certain excessively rigid schemata—for example, the distinction between the *teaching* Church and the *learning* Church must take into consideration the fact that each of the baptized participates, albeit at his own level, in the prophetic, priestly, and kingly mission of Christ. *Therefore we are talking not only about changing concepts but also of renewing attitudes*, as I tried to show in the book I wrote after the Council, *Sources of Renewal*.

But let me return for a moment to the current religious situation in Europe. Some hoped that after the fall of Communism there would have been an *instinctive turn toward religion* at all levels of society. Did this happen? It certainly did not happen in the way some had imagined; but nevertheless we can affirm that it is happening, especially in Russia. How? Above all in the return to the traditions and practices of the Orthodox Church. In those regions, moreover, thanks to the restoration of religious freedom, there also has been a rebirth of the Catholic Church, which had been present for centuries through the Poles, the Germans, the Lithuanians, and the Ukrainians living in Russia. Protestant communities and numerous *Western sects,* with great economic resources at their disposal, are also enjoying a renewal there.

In other countries the return to religion, or perseverance in one's own Church, occurs in direct relation to the Church's actual experience during the Communist oppression, as well as in relation to older traditions. This is the case in societies like Bohemia, Slovakia, Hungary, and even predominantly Orthodox countries like Romania or Bulgaria. The former Yugoslavian and Baltic countries present their own particular problems.

Where does the true power of the Church lie? Naturally, over the centuries in the West and the East the power of the Church has lain in the witness of the *saints,* of those who made Christ's truth their own truth, who followed the way that is Christ Himself and who lived the life that flows from Him in the Holy Spirit. And in the Eastern and Western Churches these saints have never been lacking.

The saints of our century have been in large part martyrs. The totalitarian regimes which dominated Europe in the middle of the twentieth century added to their numbers. Concentration camps, death camps—which produced, among other things, the monstrous Holocaust of the Jews—revealed authentic saints among Catholics and Orthodox, and among Protestants as well. These were true martyrs. It is enough to recall such figures as Father Maximilian Kolbe and Edith Stein and, even earlier, the martyrs of the Spanish Civil War.

In eastern Europe the army of holy martyrs, especially among the Orthodox, is enormous: Russians, Ukrainians, Byelorussians, and those from the vast territories beyond the Ural Mountains. There were also Catholic martyrs in Russia, in Byelorussia, in Lithuania, in the Baltic countries, in the Balkans, in the Ukraine, in Galicia, Romania, Bulgaria, Albania, and in the countries of the former Yugoslavia. This is the great multitude of those who, as is said in the Book of Revelation, "follow the Lamb" (cf. Rev 14:4). They have completed in their death as martyrs the redemptive sufferings of Christ (cf. Col 1:24) and, at the same time, they have become *the foundation of a new world, a new Europe, and a new civilization.*

DOES "ETERNAL LIFE" EXIST?

RECENTLY IN THE CHURCH, WORDS HAVE MULTI-plied. It seems that in the last twenty years more "documents" have been produced at every level of the Church than in the entire preceding twenty centuries.

Yet to some it has seemed that this very loquacious Church is silent about what is most essential: eternal life.

Your Holiness, do heaven, purgatory, and hell still exist? Why do many Churchmen comment interminably upon topical issues, but hardly ever speak to us about eternity, about that ultimate union with God that, as faith teaches, remains man's vocation, man's destiny, and ultimate end?

PLEASE OPEN THE DOGMATIC CONSTITUTION ON the Church, *Lumen Gentium*, to chapter 7, which discusses the eschatological character of the pilgrim Church on earth, as well as the union of the earthly

Church with the Church in heaven. Your question addresses not the unity of the pilgrim Church and the heavenly Church, but the connection between eschatology and the Church on earth. In this regard, you point out that in pastoral practice this perspective has in some ways been lost, and I must acknowledge that there is some truth to this.

Let's remember that not so long ago, in sermons during retreats or missions, the *Last Things*—death, judgment, heaven, hell, and purgatory—were always a standard part of the program of meditation and preachers knew how to speak of them in an effective and evocative way. How many people were drawn to conversion and confession by these sermons and reflections on the Last Things!

Furthermore, we have to recognize that this pastoral style was *profoundly personal:* "Remember that at the end you will present yourself before God with your entire life. Before His judgment seat you will be responsible for all of your actions, you will be judged not only on your actions and on your words but also on your thoughts, even the most secret." It could be said that these sermons, which correspond perfectly to the content of Revelation in the Old and New Testaments, went to the very heart of man's inner world. They stirred his conscience, they threw him to his knees, they led him to the screen of the confessional, they had a profound saving effect all their own.

. . .

Man is free and therefore *responsible*. His is a personal and social responsibility, a responsibility before God, a responsibility which is his greatness. I understand the fears of which you are speaking: you are afraid that the fact that one no longer speaks of these things in evangelization, in catechesis, and in homilies represents a *threat to this basic greatness of man*. Indeed, we could ask ourselves if the Church would still be able to awaken heroism and produce saints without proclaiming this message. And I am not speaking so much about the "great" saints, who are elevated to the honor of the altars, but of the "everyday" saints, to use the term in the sense it has had from early Christian literature.

Significantly, the Council also reminds us of the universal call to holiness in the Church. This vocation is universal and concerns each of the baptized, every Christian. It is always very personal, connected to work, to one's profession. It is an account rendered of the talents each person has received—whether one has made good or bad use of them. We know that the words the Lord Jesus spoke about the man who had buried the talent were very harsh and threatening (cf. Mt 25:25–30).

It can be said that until recently the Church's catechesis and preaching centered upon an *individual eschatology*, one, for that matter, which is profoundly rooted in Divine Revelation. The vision proposed by the Council, however, was that of an *eschatology of the Church and of the world*.

The title of chapter 7 of *Lumen Gentium*—"The Eschatological Nature of the Pilgrim Church"—which I suggested you reread, clearly reveals this intention. Here is the opening passage: "The Church, to which we are all called in Jesus Christ and in which through God's grace we attain holiness, will reach its fulfillment only in the glory of heaven, when the time comes for the renewal of all things (cf. Acts 3:21), and when the human race together with the entire world, which is intimately connected to man and through him arrives at its destiny, will be perfectly renewed in Christ. . . . And indeed Christ, when He rose up from the earth, drew all to Himself (cf. Jn 12:32); rising from the dead (cf. Rm 6:9) He instilled in the Apostles His animating Spirit, and through the Spirit built His Body which is the Church, the universal sacrament of salvation; seated at the right hand of the Father, He is continually at work in the world guiding men to the Church and through it uniting them more closely with Himself, and nourishing them with His own Body and Blood He gives them a share in His glorious life. Therefore, the promised renewal that we await is already begun in Christ. It is carried forward by the Holy Spirit and through the Spirit it continues in the Church, where the faith teaches us the meaning of our temporal life, while we finish, in the hope of future good, the work given to us in the world by the Father, and thus give fulfillment to our salvation (cf. Phil 2:12). The end of the age has already arrived (cf. 1 Cor 10:11) and the world's renewal is irrevocably set—and in a certain real way it is even anticipated in this world. Already, on earth the Church is adorned with true, even if imperfect, holiness. But until there are new heavens and a new earth, in which justice resides (cf. 2 Pt 3:10–13), the pilgrim Church, with its sacraments and institutions which belong to the present stage of history, carries the mark of this fleeting world, and lives among creation, which still groans and struggles, yearning for the appearance of the children of God (cf. Rm 8:19–22)" (*Lumen Gentium* 48).

It must be admitted that *this eschatological vision was only faintly present in traditional preaching.* And yet we are talking about an original, biblical vision. The entire passage I just quoted is actually composed of passages cited from the Gospel, the letters of the Apostles, and the Acts of the Apostles. The eschatological tradition, which centered upon the so-called *Last Things,* is placed by the Council in this fundamental biblical vision. Eschatology, as I have already mentioned, is *profoundly anthropological,* but in light of the New Testament, it is above all centered on Christ and the Holy Spirit, and it is also, in a certain sense, *cosmic.*

We can ask ourselves if man, with his individual life, his responsibility, his destiny, with his personal eschatological future, his heaven or hell or purgatory, does not end up getting lost in this cosmic dimension. Recognizing the good reasons which led you to ask your question, it is necessary to respond honestly by saying yes: *To a certain degree man does get lost;* so too do preachers, catechists, teachers; and as a result, they no longer have the courage to preach the threat of hell. And perhaps even those who listen to them have stopped being afraid of hell.

In fact, *people of our time have become insensitive to the Last Things.* On the one hand, *secularization and secularism* promote this insensitivity and lead to a consumer mentality oriented toward the enjoyment of earthly goods. On the other hand, the *"hells on earth"* created in this century which is now drawing to a close have also contributed to this insensitivity. After the experience of concentration camps, gulags, bombings, not to mention natural catastrophes, can man possibly expect anything worse from this world, an even greater amount of humiliation and contempt? In a word, hell?

To a certain degree, eschatology has become irrelevant to contemporary man, especially in our civilization. Nonetheless, *faith in God, as Supreme Justice,* has not become irrelevant to man; the expectation remains that there is Someone who, in the end, will be able to speak the truth about the good and evil which man does, Someone able to reward the good and punish the bad. No one else but He is capable of doing it. People continue to have this awareness, which has survived in spite of the horrors of our century. "And so it is appointed that men die once, and then comes judgment" (cf. Heb 9:27).

This awareness also represents, in a certain sense, a common denominator for all monotheistic religions as well as for others. When the Council speaks of the eschatological character of the pilgrim Church it does so on the basis of this awareness. *God, who is the just Judge,* the Judge who rewards good and punishes evil, is none other than the God of Abraham, of Isaac, of Moses, and also of Christ, who is His Son. This God is, *above all, Love.* Not just Mercy, but Love. Not only the Father of the prodigal son, but the Father who "gave his only Son, so that everyone who believes in him might not perish but might have eternal life" (cf. Jn 3:16).

This truth which the Gospel teaches about God requires a certain *change in focus with regard to eschatology.* First of all, eschatology is not what will take place in the future, something happening only after earthly life is finished. *Eschatology has already begun with the coming of Christ.* The ultimate eschatological event was His redemptive Death and His Resurrection. This is the beginning of "a new heaven and a new earth" (cf. Rev 21:1). For everyone, life beyond death is connected with the affirmation: "I believe in the resurrection of the body," and then: "I believe in the forgiveness of sins and in life everlasting." This is *Christocentric eschatology.*

In Christ, God revealed to the world that He desires "everyone to be saved and to come to knowledge of the truth" (1 Tm 2:4). This phrase from the First Letter to

Timothy is of fundamental importance for understanding and preaching the Last Things. If God desires this— if, for this reason, God has given His Son, who in turn is at work in the Church through the Holy Spirit—*can man be damned,* can he be rejected by God?

The problem of hell has always disturbed great thinkers in the Church, beginning with Origen and continuing in our time with Sergey Bulgakov and Hans Urs von Balthasar. In point of fact, the ancient councils rejected the theory of the *"final apocatastasis,"* according to which the world would be regenerated after destruction, and every creature would be saved; a theory which indirectly abolished hell. But the problem remains. Can God, who has loved man so much, permit the man who rejects Him to be condemned to eternal torment? And yet, the words of Christ are unequivocal. In Matthew's Gospel He speaks clearly of those who will go to eternal punishment (cf. Mt 25:46). Who will these be? The Church has never made any pronouncement in this regard. This is a mystery, truly inscrutable, which embraces the holiness of God and the conscience of man. The silence of the Church is, therefore, the only appropriate position for Christian faith. Even when Jesus says of Judas, the traitor, "It would be better for that man if he had never been born" (Mt 26:24), His words do not allude for certain to eternal damnation.

At the same time, however, there is something in man's moral conscience itself that rebels against any loss of this conviction: Is not God who is Love also ultimate Justice? Can He tolerate these terrible crimes, can they go unpunished? Isn't final punishment in some way necessary in order to reestablish moral equilibrium in the complex history of humanity? Is not hell in a certain sense the ultimate safeguard of man's moral conscience?

The Holy Scriptures include the concept of the *purifying fire*. The Eastern Church adopted it because it was biblical, while not receiving the Catholic doctrine on purgatory.

Besides the bull of Benedict XII from the fourteenth century, the *mystical works of Saint John of the Cross* offered me a very strong argument for purgatory. The "living flame of love," of which Saint John speaks, is above all a purifying fire. The mystical nights described by this great Doctor of the Church on the basis of his own experience correspond, in a certain sense, to purgatory. God makes man pass through such an interior purgatory of his sensual and spiritual nature in order to bring him into union with Himself. Here we do not find ourselves before a mere tribunal. We present ourselves before the power of Love itself.

Before all else, it is Love that judges. God, who is Love, judges through love. It is Love that demands purification, before man can be made ready for that union with God which is his ultimate vocation and destiny.

Perhaps this is enough. Many theologians, in the East and the West, including contemporary theologians, have devoted their studies to the Last Things. The

Church still has its eschatological awareness. It still leads man to eternal life. If the Church should cease to do so, it would cease being faithful to its vocation, to the New Covenant, which God has made with it in Jesus Christ.

What Is the Use of
Believing?

TODAY, MANY WHO HAVE BEEN FORMED—OR deformed—by a sort of pragmatism and a utilitarianism, seem to ask: "When all is said and done, what is the use of believing? Does faith offer something more? Isn't it possible to live an honest upright life without bothering to take the Gospel seriously?"

———

TO SUCH A QUESTION ONE COULD RESPOND very succinctly: *The usefulness of faith is not comparable to any good, not even one of a moral nature.* The Church, in fact, has never denied that even a nonbeliever could perform good and noble actions. Everyone can easily agree with this. The value of faith cannot be explained, even though efforts are often made to do so, by merely stressing its usefulness for human morality. Rather, one could say that *the basic usefulness of faith lies precisely in the fact that a person believes and entrusts him-*

self. By believing and entrusting ourselves, in fact, we respond to God's word. His word does not fall into a void, but returns to Him, having borne fruit, as was said very effectively in the Book of Isaiah (cf. Is 55:11). Nevertheless, God absolutely does not want to force us to respond to His word.

In this regard, the Council's teaching, and especially the Declaration on Religious Freedom, *Dignitatis Humanae,* is particularly important. It would be worthwhile to quote and analyze the entire Declaration. Instead, perhaps quoting a few phrases will do: "And all human beings" we read, "are bound to search for the truth, especially with regard to God and His Church, and as they come to know it they are bound to adhere to the truth and pay homage to it" (*Dignitatis Humanae* 1).

What the Council emphasizes here, above all, is the *dignity of man.* The text continues: "Motivated by their dignity, all human beings, inasmuch as they are individuals endowed with reason and free will, and thus invested with personal responsibility, are bound by both their nature and by moral duty to search for the truth, above all religious truth. And once they come to know it they are bound to adhere to it and to arrange their entire lives according to the demands of such truth" (*Dignitatis Humanae* 2). "The way in which the truth is sought, however, must be in keeping with man's dignity and his social nature—that is, by searching freely, with the help of instruction or education . . . through communication and dialogue" (*Dignitatis Humanae* 3).

. . .

As these passages show, *the Council treats human freedom very seriously* and appeals to the inner imperative of the conscience in order to demonstrate that the answer, given by man to God and to His word through faith, is closely connected with his personal dignity. *Man cannot be forced to accept the truth*. He can be drawn toward the truth only by his own nature, that is, by his own freedom, which commits him to search sincerely for truth and, when he finds it, to adhere to it both in his convictions and in his behavior.

This has always been the teaching of the Church. But even before that, it was the teaching that Christ Himself exemplified by His actions. It is from this perspective that the second part of the Council's Declaration on Religious Freedom should be reread. There, perhaps, you will find the answer to your question.

It is an answer that echoes the teaching of the Fathers and the theological tradition from Saint Thomas Aquinas to John Henry Newman. The Council merely reaffirms what has always been the Church's conviction. The position of Saint Thomas is, in fact, well known: He is so consistent in his respect for conscience that he maintains that it is wrong for one to make an act of faith in Christ if in one's conscience one is convinced, however absurdly, that it is wrong to carry out such an act (cf. *Summa Theologiae* 1–2. 19. 5). If man is admonished by his conscience—even if an erroneous conscience, but one whose voice appears to him as unquestionably true—he must always listen to it. What is not permissible is that he culpably indulge in error without trying to reach the truth.

If Newman places conscience above authority, he is not proclaiming anything new with respect to the constant teaching of the Church. The *conscience,* as the Council teaches, "is man's sanctuary and most secret core, where he finds himself alone with God, whose voice resounds within him. . . . In loyalty to conscience Christians unite with others in order to search for the truth and to resolve, according to this truth, the many moral problems which arise in the life of individuals as well as in the life of society. Therefore, the more a good conscience prevails the more people and social groups move away from blind willfulness and endeavor to conform to the objective norms of moral behavior. Nonetheless, it often happens that conscience errs through invincible ignorance, without, for this reason, losing its dignity. But this cannot be said of the man who does very little to search for truth and good, or when through the habit of sin conscience itself becomes almost blind" (*Gaudium et Spes* 16).

It is difficult not to be struck by the profound internal consistency of the Council's Declaration on Religious Freedom. In the light of its teaching, we can say that *the essential usefulness of faith consists in the fact that, through faith, man achieves the good of his rational nature.* And he achieves it by giving his response to God, as is his duty—a duty not only to God, but also to himself.

Christ did everything in order to convince us of the importance of this response. Man is called upon to give this response with inner freedom so that it will radiate that *veritatis splendor* so essential to human dignity. Christ committed the Church to act in the same way. This is why its history is so full of protests against all those who attempted to force faith, "making conversions by the sword." In this regard, it must be remembered that the Spanish theologians in Salamanca took a clear stance in opposition to violence committed against the native peoples of America, the *indios*, under the pretext of converting them to Christianity. Even earlier, in the same spirit the Academy of Kraków issued at the Council of Constance in 1414 a condemnation of the violence perpetrated against the Baltic peoples under a similar pretext.

Christ certainly desires faith. He desires it *of man* and he desires it *for man.* To people seeking miracles from Him He would respond: "Your faith has saved you" (cf. Mk 10:52). The case of the Canaanite woman is particularly touching. At first it seems as if Jesus does not want to hear her request that He help her daughter, almost as if he wanted to provoke her moving profession of faith "For even the dogs eat the scraps that fall from the table of their masters" (Mt 15:27). He puts the foreign woman to the test in order to be able then to say: "Great is your faith! Let it be done for you as you wish" (Mt 15:28).

Christ wants to awaken faith in human hearts. He wants them to respond to the word of the Father, but He wants this in full respect for human dignity. In the very search for faith an implicit faith is already present, and therefore the necessary condition for salvation is already satisfied.

From this point of view your question finds a rather complete response in the words of the Council's Constitution on the Church. Therefore it deserves to be read once again: "In fact, those who through no fault of their own are not aware of the Gospel of Christ and of the Church, but who nonetheless search sincerely for God, and with the help of grace attempt to carry out His will, known through the dictates of their conscience—they too can attain eternal salvation. Nor will Divine Providence deny the help necessary for salvation to those who have not yet arrived at a clear knowledge and recognition of God, and who attempt, not without divine grace, to conduct a good life" (*Lumen Gentium* 16).

In your question you speak of "an honest, upright life even without the Gospel." I would respond that if a life is truly upright it is because the Gospel, not known and therefore not rejected on a conscious level, is in reality already at work in the depths of the person who searches for the truth with honest effort and who willingly accepts it as soon as it becomes known to him.

Such willingness is, in fact, a manifestation of grace at work in the soul. The Spirit blows where He wills and as He wills (cf. Jn 3:8). *The freedom of the Spirit meets the freedom of man and fully confirms it.*

This clarification was necessary in order to avoid any danger of a *Pelagian interpretation.* This danger already existed in the time of Saint Augustine, and seems to be surfacing again in our time. Pelagius asserted that even without divine grace, man could lead a good and happy life. Divine grace, therefore, was not necessary for him. But the truth is that man is actually called to salvation; that a good life is the condition of salvation; and that salvation cannot be attained without the help of grace.

Ultimately, only God can save man, but He expects man to cooperate. The fact that man can cooperate with God determines his authentic greatness. The truth according to which man is called to cooperate with God in all things, with a view toward the ultimate purpose of his life—his salvation and divinization—found expression in the Eastern tradition in the doctrine of *synergism.* With God, man "creates" the world; *with God, man "creates" his personal salvation.* The divinization of man comes from God. But here, too, man must cooperate with God.

Human Rights

A GAIN YOU REFER TO HUMAN DIGNITY. Together with human rights, which are a consequence of human dignity, this is one of the central and
recurring subjects of your teaching. But what does the
Holy Father really mean by "human dignity"? What is
his understanding of authentic "human rights"? Concessions from governments and states? Or something
quite different, something much more profound?

I N A CERTAIN SENSE I HAVE ALREADY ADDRESSED
the problem at the heart of your question: "What
does human dignity mean? What are the human
rights?" It is evident that these rights were inscribed by
the Creator in the order of creation; so we cannot speak
of concessions on the part of human institutions, on
the part of states and international organizations.

These institutions express no more than what God Himself inscribed in the order He created, what He Himself has inscribed in the moral conscience, or in the human heart, as Saint Paul explains in the Letter to the Romans (cf. Rom 2:15).

The Gospel is the fullest confirmation of all of human rights. Without it we can easily find ourselves far from the truth about man. The Gospel, in fact, confirms the divine rule which upholds the moral order of the universe and confirms it, particularly through the Incarnation itself. Who is man, if the Son took on human nature? Who must this man be, if the Son of God pays the supreme price for his dignity? Every year the Church's liturgy expresses its profound wonder as it contemplates this truth and this mystery, both at Christmas and during the Easter Vigil. *"O felix culpa, quae talem ac tantum meruit habere Redemptorem"* ("Oh happy fault, which gained for us so great a Redeemer!" *Exultet*). *The Redeemer confirms human rights* simply by restoring the fullness of the dignity man received when God created him in His image and likeness.

Since you have touched upon this problem, let me take advantage of your question to recall how this issue gradually came to be *so central for me.* In a certain sense it was a great surprise for me to realize that interest in man and in his dignity had become, despite expectations to the contrary, the principal theme of the *polemic*

against Marxism, and this because the Marxists themselves had made the question of man the center of their
arguments.

After the war, when the Marxists seized power in
Poland and began to control the university curriculum,
one might have expected that initially its program of
dialectical materialism would be expressed, above all,
through *natural philosophy.* It should be said that the
Church in Poland was prepared for this. In the years following the war, I remember what a comfort the writings
of Father Kazimierz Kłósak—a distinguished professor
in the Faculty of Theology in Kraków known for his
extraordinary erudition—represented for Catholic intellectuals. In Kłósak's scholarly writings, Marxist natural
philosophy was challenged by an innovative approach
that allowed for the discovery of the Logos—creative
thought and order—in the world. Thus Kłósak became a
part of the philosophical tradition that started with the
Greek thinkers, continued through the *quinque viae* of
Saint Thomas, and even in such contemporary scientists
as Alfred North Whitehead.

The visible world, in and of itself, cannot offer a scientific basis for an atheistic interpretation of reality.
Instead, honest reflection does find sufficient elements
in the world to arrive at the knowledge of God. In this
sense the atheistic interpretation of reality is one-sided
and tendentious.

I still remember those discussions. I also participated
in many meetings with scientists, in particular with

physicists, who, after Einstein, were quite open to a theistic interpretation of the world.

But oddly enough, this kind of controversy with Marxism was brief. It soon came about that man himself—and his moral life—was the *central problem under discussion*. Natural philosophy was, so to speak, put aside. In attempting an apologia of atheism, the discussion of ethics soon superseded the interpretation of the physical world. When I wrote the book *The Acting Person*, the first to take notice of it, obviously in order to attack it, were the Marxists. In fact, my book represented an unsettling element in their polemic against religion and the Church.

But, having arrived at this point, I must say that my concern for "the acting person" did not arise from the disputes with Marxism or, at least, not as a direct response to those disputes. I had long been interested in *man as person*. Perhaps my interest was due to the fact that I had never had a particular predilection for the natural sciences. I was always more fascinated by man. While studying in the Faculty of Literature, man interested me inasmuch as he was a creator of language and a subject of literature; then, when I discovered my priestly vocation, man became the *central theme of my pastoral work*.

By this point the war had ended and the controversies with Marxism were in full swing. In those years, my greatest involvement was with young people who asked me questions, not so much about the existence of God, but rather *about how to live,* how to face and resolve problems of love and marriage, not to mention problems related to work. The memory of those young people from the period following the German occupation has always remained with me. In a certain sense, with their doubts and with their questions, they also showed me the way. From our meetings, from my sharing in the problems of their lives, a book was born, the contents of which is summarized in the title *Love and Responsibility.*

My book on the acting person came later, but it was also born of the same source. In some ways it was inevitable that I would arrive at this theme from the moment I began to deal with questions concerning human existence—questions asked by people not only in our time but in every time. The question of good and evil is always with us, as shown by the young man in the Gospel who asks Jesus: "What must I do to inherit eternal life?" (Mk 10:17).

So the development of my studies centered on man—on the human person—can ultimately be explained by my *pastoral concern.* And it is precisely from a pastoral point of view that, in *Love and Responsibility,* I formulated the concept of a *personalistic principle.* This principle is an attempt to translate the commandment of love into the language of philosophical ethics. *The person is a being for whom the only suitable dimension is love.* We are just to a person if we love him.

This is as true for God as it is for man. Love for a person *excludes the possibility of treating him as an object of pleasure.* This is a principle of Kantian ethics and constitutes his so-called second imperative. This imperative, however, is negative in character and does not exhaust the entire content of the commandment of love. If Kant so strongly emphasized that the person cannot be treated as an object of pleasure, he did so in order to oppose Anglo-Saxon utilitarianism, and from this point of view, he achieved his goal. Nevertheless, Kant did not fully interpret the commandment of love. In fact, the commandment of love is not limited to excluding all behavior that reduces the person to a mere object of pleasure. It requires more; it requires the *affirmation of the person as a person.*

The true personalistic interpretation of the commandment of love is found in the words of the Council: "When the Lord Jesus prays to the Father so that 'they may be one' (Jn 17:22), He places before us new horizons impervious to human reason and implies a similarity between the union of divine persons and the union of the children of God in truth and charity. This similarity shows how man, who is the only creature on earth that God wanted for his own sake, can fully discover himself only by the sincere giving of himself" (*Gaudium et Spes* 24). Here we truly have an adequate interpretation of the commandment of love. Above all, *the principle that a person has value by the simple fact that he is a person* finds very clear expression: man, it is said, "is the only creature on earth that God has wanted for his own sake." At the same time the Council emphasizes that the most important thing about love is the sincere gift of self. In this sense *the person is realized through love.*

Therefore, these two aspects—the affirmation of the person as a person and the sincere gift of self—not only do not exclude each other, they mutually confirm and complete each other. *Man affirms himself most completely by giving of himself.* This is the fufillment of the commandment of love. This is also the full truth about man, a truth that Christ taught us by His life, and that the tradition of Christian morality, no less than the tradition of saints and of the many heroes of love of neighbor, took up and lived out in the course of history.

If we deprive *human freedom* of this possibility, if man does not commit himself to becoming a gift for others, then this freedom can become dangerous. It will become freedom to do what I myself consider as good, what brings me a profit or pleasure, even a sublimated pleasure. *If we cannot accept the prospect of giving ourselves as a gift, then the danger of a selfish freedom will always be present.* Kant fought against this danger, and along the same line so did Max Scheler and so many after him who shared his ethics of values. But a complete expression of all this is already found in the Gospel. For this very reason, *we can find in the Gospel a consistent declaration of all human rights,* even those that for various reasons can make us feel uneasy.

THE DEFENSE
OF EVERY LIFE

AMONG THE RIGHTS YOU MENTIONED, THOSE
which might "make us uneasy," foremost is the
right to life, which must be defended from the moment
of conception. This is also an issue which is frequently
and forcefully raised in your teaching. Your repeated
condemnation of any legalization of abortion has even
been defined as "obsessive" by certain cultural and
political factions which hold that "humanitarian reasons" are on their side—the side that has led governments to permit abortion.

FOR MAN, THE RIGHT TO LIFE IS THE
fundamental right. And yet, a part of contemporary
culture has wanted to deny that right, turning it into an
"uncomfortable" right, one that has to be defended. But
there is no other right that so closely affects the very
existence of the person! The right to life means the right

to be born and then continue to live until one's natural end: "As long as I live, I have the right to live."

The question of conceived and unborn children is a particularly delicate yet clear problem. The *legalization of the termination of pregnancy* is none other than the authorization given to an adult, with the approval of an established law, to take the lives of children yet unborn and thus incapable of defending themselves. It is difficult to imagine a more unjust situation, and *it is very difficult to speak of obsession in a matter such as this,* where we are dealing with a fundamental imperative of every good conscience—the defense of the right to life of an innocent and defenseless human being.

Often the question is presented as a woman's right to *free choice* regarding the life already existing inside her, that she carries in her womb: the woman should have the right to choose between giving life or taking it away from the unborn child. Anyone can see that *the alternative here is only apparent. It is not possible to speak of the right to choose when a clear moral evil is involved,* when what is at stake is the commandment *Do not kill!*

Might this commandment allow of *exception?* The answer in and of itself is no, since even the hypothesis of *legitimate defense,* which never concerns an innocent but always and only an unjust aggressor, must respect the principle that moralists call the *principium inculpatae tutelae* (the principle of nonculpable defense). In order to be legitimate, that "defense" must be carried out in a way that causes the least damage and, if possible, saves the life of the aggressor.

This is not the case with an unborn child. *A child conceived in its mother's womb is never an unjust aggressor;* it is a defenseless being that is waiting to be welcomed and helped.

It is necessary to recognize that, in this context, we are witnessing true human tragedies. Often *the woman is the victim of male selfishness,* in the sense that the man, who has contributed to the conception of the new life, does not want to be burdened with it and leaves the responsibility to the woman, as if it were "her fault" alone. So, precisely when the woman most needs the man's support, he proves to be a cynical egotist, capable of exploiting her affection or weakness, yet stubbornly resistant to any sense of responsibility for his own action. These are problems that are well known not only in confessionals, but also in courts throughout the world and, more and more these days, in courts that deal with minors.

Therefore, *in firmly rejecting "pro choice" it is necessary to become courageously "pro woman," promoting a choice that is truly in favor of women.* It is precisely the woman, in fact, who pays the highest price, not only for her motherhood, but even more for its destruction, for the suppression of the life of the child who has been conceived. The only honest stance, in these cases, *is that of radical solidarity with the woman.* It is not right to leave her alone. The experiences of many counseling centers show that the woman does not want to suppress the life of the child she carries within her. If she is supported in this attitude, and if at the same time she is freed from the intimidation of those around her, then she is even capable of heroism. As I have said, numerous counseling centers are witness to this, as are, in a special way, houses for teenage mothers. It seems, therefore, that society is beginning to develop a more mature attitude in this regard, even if there are still many self-styled "benefactors" who claim to "help" women by liberating them from the prospect of motherhood.

We find ourselves here before a *very delicate situation,* both from the point of view of human rights and from a moral and pastoral point of view. All of these aspects are intertwined. *I have always observed this to be the case in my own life and in my ministry* as a priest, as a diocesan bishop, and then as the successor to Peter, with all the responsibility that this office entails.

Therefore, I must repeat that *I categorically reject every accusation or suspicion concerning the Pope's alleged "obsession" with this issue.* We are dealing with a problem of tremendous importance, in which all of us must show the utmost responsibility and vigilance. *We cannot afford forms of permissiveness* that would lead directly to the trampling of human rights, and also to the complete destruction of values which are fundamental not only for the lives of individuals and families but for society itself. Isn't there a sad truth in the powerful expression *culture of death?*

Obviously, the opposite of the culture of death is not and cannot be a program of irresponsible global population growth. *The rate of population growth needs to be taken into consideration.* The right path is that which the Church calls *responsible parenthood;* this is taught by the Church's family counseling programs. *Responsible parenthood is the necessary condition for human love, and it is also the necessary condition for authentic conjugal love,* because love cannot be irresponsible. Its beauty is the fruit of responsibility. When love is truly responsible, it is also truly free.

This is precisely the teaching I learned from the encyclical *Humanae Vitae* written by my venerable predecessor Paul VI, and that I had learned even earlier *from my young friends, married and soon to be married,* while I was writing *Love and Responsibility.* As I have said, they themselves were my teachers in this area. It was they, men and women alike, who made a creative contribution to the pastoral care of family, to pastoral efforts on behalf of responsible parenthood, to the foundation of counseling programs, which subsequently flourished. The principal activity and primary commitment of these programs is to foster human love. In them, *responsibility for human love* has been and continues to be lived out.

The hope is that *this responsibility will never be lacking in any place or in any person;* that this responsibility will never be lacking in legislators, teachers, or pastors. How many little-known people there are whom I would like to mention here and express my deepest gratitude for their generous commitment and great dedication! In their lives we find confirmation of the Christian and of the personalistic truth about man, who becomes fully himself to the extent that he gives himself as a free gift to others.

From the counseling programs we must turn to the *universities.* I have in mind the schools that I know and the institutions to whose founding I have contributed. I am thinking here in particular of the chair of ethics at the *Catholic University of Lublin,* as well as the institute erected there after my departure, under the direction of my closest collaborators and disciples—in particular Father Tadeusz Styczeń and Father Andrzej Szostek. The concept of "person" is not only a marvelous theory; it is at the center of the human *ethos.*

I must also recall the analogous institute created at the *Lateran University* in Rome, which has already been the inspiration for similar initiatives in the United States, in Mexico, in Chile, and in other countries. The most effective way to be at the service of the truth of responsible parenthood is to show its ethical and anthropological foundations. In this field more than in any other, collaboration among pastors, biologists, and physicians is indispensable.

. . .

I cannot dwell here on *contemporary thinkers,* but I must mention at least one name—*Emmanuel Lévinas,* who represents a particular school of contemporary *personalism* and of the *philosophy of dialogue.* Like Martin Buber and Franz Rosenzweig, he takes up the personalistic tradition of the Old Testament, where the relationship between the human "I" and the divine, absolutely sovereign "THOU" is so heavily emphasized.

God, who is the supreme Legislator, forcefully enjoined on Sinai the commandment "Thou shalt not kill," as an absolute moral imperative. Lévinas, who, like his co-religionists, deeply experienced the tragedy of the Holocaust, offers a remarkable formulation of this fundamental commandment of the Decalogue— for him, the face reveals the person. This *philosophy of the face* is also found in the *Old Testament,* in the Psalms, and in the writings of the Prophets: there are frequent references to "seeking God's Face" (cf. Ps 26[27]:8). It is through his face that man speaks, and in particular, every man who has suffered a wrong speaks and says the words "Do not kill me!" *The human face and the commandment "Do not kill" are ingeniously joined in Lévinas, and thus become a testimony for our age,* in which governments, even democratically elected governments, sanction executions with such ease.

Perhaps it is better to say no more than this about such a painful subject.

THE MOTHER
OF GOD

THE RENEWAL OF MARIAN THEOLOGY AND devotion—in continuity with Catholic tradition—is another distinctive characteristic of the teaching and pastoral activity of John Paul II. *Totus Tuus* ("I am completely yours, O Mary") is the motto you chose for your papacy.

Furthermore, for some time now there have been rumors and reports of mysterious apparitions and messages of the Virgin Mary; as in earlier centuries, crowds of people are setting out on pilgrimage. Your Holiness, what can you tell us about this?

TOTUS TUUS. THIS PHRASE IS NOT ONLY AN expression of piety, or simply an expression of devotion. It is more. During the Second World War, while I was employed as a factory worker, I came to be attracted to Marian devotion. At first, it had seemed to me that I should distance myself a bit from the Marian devotion of my childhood, in order to focus more on Christ. Thanks to Saint Louis of Montfort, I came to understand that true *devotion to the Mother of God is actually Christocentric, indeed, it is very profoundly rooted in the Mystery of the Blessed Trinity,* and the mysteries of the Incarnation and Redemption.

And so, I rediscovered Marian piety, this time with a deeper understanding. This mature form of devotion to the Mother of God has stayed with me over the years, bearing fruit in the encyclicals *Redemptoris Mater* and *Mulieris Dignitatem.*

In regard to Marian devotion, each of us must understand that such devotion not only addresses a need of the heart, a sentimental inclination, but that it also corresponds to the objective truth about the Mother of God. Mary is the new Eve, placed by God in close relation to Christ, the new Adam, beginning with the Annunciation, through the night of His birth in Bethlehem, through the wedding feast at Cana of Galilee, through the Cross at Calvary, and up to the gift of the Holy Spirit at Pentecost. The Mother of Christ the Redeemer is the Mother of the Church.

The Second Vatican Council made great strides forward with regard to both Marian doctrine and devotion. It is impossible to include here in its entirety the marvelous eighth chapter of the Dogmatic Constitution on the Church *Lumen Gentium,* but it should be done. When I participated in the Council, I found reflected in this chapter all my earlier youthful experiences, as well as those special bonds which continue to unite me to the Mother of God in ever new ways.

The *first way*—and the oldest—is tied to all the times during my childhood that I stopped before the image of Our Lady of Perpetual Help in the parish church of Wadowice. It is tied to the tradition of the Carmelite scapular, rich in meaning and symbolism, which I knew from my youth through the Carmelite convent "on the hill" in my home town. It is also tied to the *tradition of making pilgrimages to the shrine of Kalwaria Zebrzydowska,* one of those places that draws crowds of pilgrims, especially from the south of Poland and from beyond the Carpathian Mountains. This local shrine is remarkable because it is not only Marian but also profoundly focused on Christ. During their stay at the shrine of Kalwaria, the first thing the pilgrims do is to make their way along a Via Crucis (Way of the Cross) in which, through Mary, humanity finds its rightful place alongside Christ. The Crucifix stands at the top of a hill dominating the entire area around the sanctuary. The solemn Marian procession, which takes place before the solemnity of the Assumption, is nothing else but the expression of faith of the Christian people that the Mother of God shares in a unique way in the Resurrection and in the Glory of her own Son.

From my earliest years, my own devotion to Mary was deeply joined to my faith in Christ. The shrine of Kalwaria helped me greatly in this.

. . .

Another chapter in my life is *Jasna Góra,* with its icon of the Black Madonna. Our Lady of Jasna Góra has been venerated for centuries as the Queen of Poland. This shrine belongs to the entire country. The Polish nation has sought for centuries, and continues to seek, support and strength for spiritual rebirth from its Lady and Queen. At Jasna Góra a special evangelization comes about. The great events in the life of Poland have always been tied to this place in some way. Both the ancient and modern history of my nation have their deepest roots there on the hill of Jasna Góra.

I think what I have said sufficiently explains the Marian devotion of the present Pope and, above all, his attitude of total *abandonment to Mary*—his *Totus Tuus.*

WOMEN

IN THE APOSTOLIC LETTER SIGNIFICANTLY entitled *Mulieris Dignitatem* (*The Dignity of Woman*), you have shown, among other things, how the veneration given by Catholics to one woman, Mary, is not at all irrelevant to the question of womanhood.

TAKING UP MY PRECEDING OBSERVATIONS, I would like to call attention again to one aspect of Marian devotion. This devotion is not only a form of piety; it is also an *attitude—an attitude toward woman as woman.*

If our century has been characterized in liberal societies by a growing *feminism,* it might be said that this trend is *a reaction to the lack of respect accorded each woman.* Everything that I have written on this theme in *Mulieris Dignitatem* I have felt since I was very young, and, in a certain sense, from infancy. Perhaps I was also influenced by the climate of the time in which I was brought up—it was a time of great respect and consideration for women, especially for women who were mothers.

I think that a certain *contemporary feminism* finds its roots in the absence of true respect for woman. Revealed truth teaches us something different. Respect for woman, amazement at the mystery of womanhood, and finally the nuptial love of God Himself and of Christ, as expressed in the Redemption, are all elements that have never been completely absent in the faith and life of the Church. This can be seen in a rich tradition of customs and practices that, regrettably, is nowadays being eroded. In our civilization woman has become, before all else, an object of pleasure.

It is very significant, on the other hand, that in the midst of this very situation the authentic *theology of woman* is being reborn. The spiritual beauty, the particular genius, of women is being rediscovered. The bases for the consolidation of the position of women in life, not only family life but also social and cultural life, are being redefined.

And for this purpose, we must return to the figure of Mary. Mary herself and devotion to Mary, when lived out in all its fullness, become a powerful and creative inspiration.

"Be Not Afraid"

As you have recalled during our conversation, it certainly was no accident that your papacy began with a cry that had and still has profound echoes throughout the world: "Be not afraid!"

Among the possible ways to understand this exhortation, doesn't Your Holiness believe that one such understanding could be this: Many have a need to be reassured, to be told to "be not afraid" of Christ and of His Gospel, because they fear that if they return to the faith their lives will become frustrated by demands perceived as more burdensome than liberating?

When, on October 22, 1978, I said the words "Be not afraid!" in St. Peter's Square, I could not fully know how far they would take me and the entire Church. Their meaning came more from the

Holy Spirit, the Consoler promised by the Lord Jesus to His disciples, than from the man who spoke them. Nevertheless, with the passing of the years, I have recalled these words on many occasions.

The exhortation "Be not afraid!" should be interpreted as having a very broad meaning. In a certain sense *it was an exhortation addressed to all people,* an exhortation to conquer fear in the present world situation, as much in the East as in the West, as much in the North as in the South.

Have no fear of that which you yourselves have created, have no fear of all that man has produced, and that every day is becoming more dangerous for him! Finally, have no fear of yourselves!

Why should we have no fear? Because man has been redeemed by God. When pronouncing these words in St. Peter's Square, I already knew that my first encyclical and my entire papacy would be tied to the truth of the Redemption. In the Redemption we find the most profound basis for the words "Be not afraid!": "For God so loved the world that he gave his only Son" (cf. Jn 3:16). This Son is always present in the history of humanity as Redeemer. The Redemption pervades all of human history, even before Christ, and prepares its eschatological future. It is the light that "shines in the darkness, and the darkness has not overcome it" (cf. Jn 1:5). *The power of Christ's Cross and Resurrection is greater than any evil which man could or should fear.*

. . .

At this point we need once again to return to *Totus Tuus.* In your earlier question you spoke of the Mother of God and of the numerous private revelations that have taken place, especially in the last two centuries. I responded by explaining how devotion to Mary developed in my own personal life, beginning in my home town, then in the shrine of Kalwaria, and finally at Jasna Góra. *Jasna Góra became part of the history of my homeland in the seventeenth century, as a sort of "Be not afraid!" spoken by Christ through the lips of His Mother.* On October 22, 1978, when I inherited the Ministry of Peter in Rome, more than anything else, it was this experience and devotion to Mary in my native land which I carried with me.

"Be not afraid!" Christ said to the apostles (cf. Lk 24:36) and to the women (cf. Mt 28:10) after the Resurrection. According to the Gospels, these words were not addressed to Mary. Strong in her faith, she had no fear. *Mary's participation in the victory of Christ became clear to me above all from the experience of my people.* Cardinal Stefan Wyszyński told me that his predecessor, Cardinal August Hlond, had spoken these prophetic words as he was dying: "The victory, if it comes, will come through Mary." During my pastoral ministry in Poland, I saw for myself how those words were coming true.

After my election as Pope, as I became more involved in the problems of the universal Church, I came to have a similar conviction: On this universal level, if victory comes it will be brought by Mary. *Christ will conquer through her, because He wants the Church's victories now and in the future to be linked to her.*

I held this conviction even though I did not yet know very much about *Fátima*. I could see, however, that there was a certain continuity among La Salette, Lourdes, and Fátima—and, in the distant past, our Polish Jasna Góra.

And thus we come to May 13, 1981, when I was wounded by gunshots fired in St. Peter's Square. At first, I did not pay attention to the fact that the assassination attempt had occurred on the exact anniversary of the day Mary appeared to the three children at Fátima in Portugal and spoke to them the words that now, at the end of this century, seem to be close to their fulfillment.

With this event, didn't Christ perhaps say, once again, "Be not afraid"? Didn't he repeat this Easter exhortation to the Pope, to the Church, and, indirectly, to the entire human family?

At the end of the second millennium, we need, perhaps more than ever, the words of the Risen Christ: "Be not afraid!" Man who, even after the fall of Communism, has not stopped being afraid and who truly has many reasons for feeling this way, needs to hear these words. Nations need to hear them, especially those nations that have been reborn after the fall of the Communist empire, as well as those that witnessed this event from the outside. Peoples and nations of the entire world need to hear these words. *Their conscience needs to grow in the certainty that Someone exists who holds in His hands the destiny of this passing world; Someone who holds the keys to death and the netherworld* (cf. Rev 1:18); *Someone who is the Alpha and the Omega of human history* (cf. Rev 22:13)—be it the individual or collective history. And this Someone is Love (cf. 1 Jn 4:8, 16)—Love that became man, Love crucified and risen, Love unceasingly present among men. It is Eucharistic Love. It is the infinite source of communion. He alone can give the ultimate assurance when He says "Be not afraid!"

You observe that contemporary man finds it hard to return to faith because he is afraid of the moral demands that faith makes upon him. And this, to a certain degree, is the truth. *The Gospel is certainly demanding.* We know that Christ never permitted His disciples and those who listened to Him to entertain any illusions about this. On the contrary, He spared no effort in preparing them for every type of internal or external difficulty, always aware of the fact that they might well decide to abandon Him. Therefore, if He says, "Be not afraid!" He certainly does not say it in order to nullify in some way that which He has required. Rather, by these words He confirms the entire truth of the Gospel and all the demands it contains. At the same time, however, He reveals that *His demands never exceed man's abilities.* If man accepts these demands with an attitude of faith, he will also find in the grace that God never fails to give him the necessary strength to meet those demands. The world is full of proof of the saving and redemptive power that the Gospels proclaim with even greater frequency than they recall demands of the moral life. How many people there are in the world whose daily lives attest to the possibility of living out the morality of the Gospel! Experience shows that a successful human life cannot be other than a life like theirs.

To accept the Gospel's demands means to affirm all of our humanity, to see in it the beauty desired by God, while at the same time recognizing, in light of the power of God Himself, our weaknesses: "What is impossible for men is possible for God" (Lk 18:27).

These two dimensions cannot be separated: on the one hand, the moral demands God makes of man; on the other, the demands of His saving love—the gift of His grace—to which God in a certain sense has bound Himself. What else is the Redemption accomplished in Christ, if not precisely this? *God desires the salvation of man, He desires that humanity find that fulfillment to which He Himself has destined it,* and Christ has the right to say that His yoke is easy and His burden, in the end, light (cf. Mt 11:30).

It is very important to cross the threshold of hope, not to stop before it, but *to let oneself be led.* I believe that the great Polish poet Cyprian Norwid had this in mind when he expressed the ultimate meaning of the Christian life in these words: "Not with the Cross of the Savior behind you, but with your own cross behind the Savior."

There is every reason for the truth of the Cross to be called the Good News.

CROSSING THE THRESHOLD OF HOPE

HOLY FATHER, IN LIGHT OF EVERYTHING you have said to us, and for which we are grateful, must we conclude that it is truly unjustifiable—today more than ever—"to be afraid" of the God of Jesus Christ? Are we to conclude that it is really worth it all "to cross the threshold of hope," to discover that we have a Father, to rediscover that we are loved?

THE PSALMIST SAYS: "THE FEAR OF THE LORD is the beginning of wisdom" (cf. Ps 110[111]:10). Allow me to refer to these biblical words in responding to your question.

The Holy Scriptures contain an insistent exhortation to cultivate the fear of God. We are speaking here of that fear which is a *gift of the Holy Spirit*. Among the seven gifts of the Holy Spirit, indicated in the words of Isaiah (cf. Is 11:2), fear of God is listed last, but that does not mean it is the least significant, since it is precisely *fear of God that is the beginning of wisdom.* And among the gifts of the Holy Spirit, wisdom holds first place. Therefore, *we need to pray that people* everywhere and especially people in our own time *will receive the fear of God.*

From the Holy Scriptures we also know that this fear—the origin of wisdom—has nothing in common with the *fear of a slave.* It is *filial fear,* not servile fear! The Hegelian paradigm of master-slave is foreign to the Gospel. It is a paradigm drawn from a world in which God is absent. In a world in which God is truly present, in the world of divine wisdom, only filial fear can be present.

The authentic and full expression of this fear is Christ Himself. Christ wants us to have fear of all that is an offense against God. He wants this because He has come into the world in order to set man free for freedom. Man is set free through love, because love is the source *par excellence* of all that is good. This love, according to the words of Saint John, *drives out all fear* (cf. 1 Jn 4:18). Every sign of servile fear vanishes before the awesome power of the All-powerful and all-present One. Its place is taken by filial concern, in order that God's will be done on earth—that will which is the good that has in Him its origin and its ultimate fulfillment.

Thus the saints of every age are also an incarnation of the filial love of Christ, which is the source of a Franciscan love for all creatures and also of love for the saving power of the Cross, which restores to the world the balance between good and evil.

Is contemporary man truly moved by a filial fear of God, a fear that is first of all love? One might think—and there is no lack of evidence to this effect—that Hegel's paradigm of the master and the servant is more present in people's consciousness today than is wisdom, whose origin lies in the filial fear of God. The philosophy of arrogance is born of the Hegelian paradigm. The only force capable of effectively counteracting this philosophy is found in the Gospel of Christ, in which the paradigm of master-slave is radically transformed into the paradigm of *father-son.*

The father-son paradigm is ageless. It is older than human history. The "rays of fatherhood" contained in this formulation belong to the Trinitarian Mystery of God Himself, which shines forth from Him, illuminating man and his history.

This notwithstanding, as we know from Revelation, in human history the "rays of fatherhood" meet a first resistance in the obscure but real fact of original sin. *This is truly the key for interpreting reality.* Original sin is not only the violation of a positive command of God but also, and above all, a violation of *the will of God as expressed in that command. Original sin attempts, then, to abolish fatherhood,* destroying its rays which permeate the created world, placing in doubt the truth about

God who is Love and leaving man only with a sense of the master-slave relationship. As a result, the Lord appears jealous of His power over the world and over man; and consequently, man feels goaded to do battle against God. No differently than in any epoch of history, the enslaved man is driven to take sides against the master who kept him enslaved.

After all I have said, I could summarize my response in the following *paradox: In order to set contemporary man free from fear* of himself, of the world, of others, of earthly powers, of oppressive systems, in order to set him free from every manifestation of a servile fear before that "prevailing force" which believers call God, *it is necessary to pray fervently that he will bear and cultivate in his heart that true fear of God, which is the beginning of wisdom.*

This fear of God is the *saving power of the Gospel.* It is a constructive, never destructive, fear. It creates people who allow themselves to be led by responsibility, by responsible love. It creates holy men and women—true Christians—to whom the future of the world ultimately belongs. André Malraux was certainly right when he said that the twenty-first century would be the century of religion or it would not be at all.

The Pope who began his papacy with the words "Be not afraid!" tries to be completely faithful to this exhortation and is always ready to be at the service of man, nations, and humanity in the spirit of this truth of the Gospel.

BIBLICAL
INDEX

GENERAL
INDEX

Japan, 107
Jasna Góra sanctuary, 205, 210
Jaworski, Archbishop Marian,
    33
Jesus Christ, 124, 125, 149, 166
    at center of faith and life of
        the Church, 42–3
    Crucifixion, 63–4, 65
    demands made upon man,
        212–14
    eternal life and, 67, 174–5,
        177, 178
    on evangelization, 105
    faith and, 185–6
    fear and, 4–8
    fear of God and, 6–7, 215–17
    on God's love for the
        world, 52–3
    God's sacrifice of, 47, 53–4,
        59–60
    as God's self–revelation, 38–9
    on God's work in the
        world, 124
    in Islam, 89
    Last Supper, 140
    as Love, 212
    Pilate's judgment of, 62
    presence in each Christian,
        11–13
    resistance to teachings,
        anticipation of, 100,
        212–13
    Resurrection, 5, 8, 43, 68–9,
        177
    resurrection of Lazarus, 69
    on sacraments, 71–2
    as Son of God, 7, 9–12, 40–1

Jews, extermination of, *see*
    Holocaust
John XXIII, Pope, 73, 137, 141,
    157
John of the Cross, Saint, 17,
    83–4, 124, 137, 179
John Paul II, Pope
    assassination attempt, 127,
        211
    "Be not afraid!" exhorta-
        tion, 4–5, 208–10, 218
    childhood of, 93
    encyclicals of, 46, 126, 165,
        166, 203
    human rights, concern
        regarding, 188–93
    inauguration as Pope, 121
    Islam, personal experience
        with, 89, 90–91
    Judaism, personal experi-
        ence with, 93–96
    Marian devotion of, 202–3,
        204, 205, 210–11
    Morocco, visit to, 91
    Poland, visit to, 54
    religious leaders, meetings
        with, 78, 82, 90, 143
    right to life, "obsession"
        with, 195, 198–9
    at Second Vatican Council,
        151–3
    synagogue of Rome, visit
        to, 95
    true worship of God, 137–8
    women, respect for, 206–7
    young people and, 115–17,
        118–22, 192

Transfiguration, the, 72
truth about ourselves, 5–6
Tyranowski, Jan, 137

Union of Brest–Litovsk (1596),
    140
Unitatis Redintegratio, 136, 141
United Nations, 120
utilitarianism, 193

Veritatis Splendor, 165, 166
Vietnam, 107
Voltaire, 49

Wadowice, Poland, 93, 94–5
Warsaw insurrection of 1944,
    115
Whitehead, Alfred North,
    190
wisdom, 215, 216, 217, 218
Wittgenstein, Ludwig, 31
women
    abortion and, 196, 197–8
    respect for, 206–7
world's reception of the
        Church's teaching, 164
    distancing from the Church,
        166

world's reception of the
        Church's teaching (*cont.*)
    faith in the Church today,
        167–8
    moral issues, 164–5
    unpopular teachings, 165–7
World War II, 93, 115
World Youth Days, 120
    1989 (Santiago de Com-
        postela), 112
    1993 (Denver), 113
worship, salvation and, 72
Wyszyński, Cardinal Stefan,
    210

young people, 114–15
    evangelism and, 108–10, 112,
        113, 119–20
    heroism of World War II
        generation, 114–15
    idealism of, 116
    John Paul II's involvement
        with, 116–21, 192
    joy and enthusiasm of,
        120–21
    love, vocation to, 117–19
    search for meaning, 116–18,
        121–2